Reading Doesn't Matter Anymore

Shattering the Myths of Literacy

David Booth

Pembroke Publishers Limited
MARKHAM, ONTARIO

Stenhouse Publishers
PORTLAND, MAINE

For Jay and Katie,
who help me read the world

© 2006 Pembroke Publishers
538 Hood Road
Markham, Ontario, Canada L3R 3K9
www.pembrokepublishers.com

Published in the U.S. by Stenhouse Publishers
480 Congress Street
Portland, ME 04101-3400
www.stenhouse.com
ISBN 13: 978-1-57110-492-2
ISBN 10: 1-57110-492-5

We acknowledge the financial support of the Government of Canada through the
Book Publishing Industry Development Program (BPIDP) for our publishing
activities.

We acknowledge the assistance of the OMDC Book Fund, an initiative of the
Ontario Media Development Corporation.

Library and Archives Canada Cataloguing in Publication

Booth, David W. (David Wallace),
 Reading doesn't matter anymore / David Booth.

ISBN 13: 978-1-55138-202-9
ISBN 10: 1-55138-202-4

 1. Reading. I. Title.

LB1050.B665 2006   428.4   C2006-902658-0

Editor: David Kilgour
Cover design: John Zehethofer
Typesetting: Jay Tee Graphics

Printed and bound in Canada
9 8 7 6 5 4 3 2 1

Contents

"Reading Doesn't Matter Anymore..."
Unless we

1. **Expand our definition of literacy.**   *5*
Dick and Jane Have Moved On • Has Anything Really
Changed? • The New Literacies • If You Don't Read Now,
You Can't Watch TV Tonight! • Who Can Read? • Reading
in the Air

2. **Include comics, magazines, poems, songs, manuals, and
novels as part of reading.**   *29*
How Comic Books Defeated School • Literacy vs. Literature •
What Book Will We Read This Year? • A Novel Defence • I'm
Not a Kid Anymore! • How Many Books Has Your Boyfriend
Read? • Do You Read Me?

3. **Understand the use of technology as literacy.**   *55*
Literacy and the Plugged-in Generation • I Liked the Movie
Better • The Mouse in Everyone's House • Mining for Gold

4. **Remember that story is the heart of literacy.**   *65*
The Tale, the Teller, the Telling, and the Told • Read Me a
Story; My Mind Is Tired • How to Read Aloud • Lattes and
Literature

5. **Help students build strong reading muscles.**   *77*
Comprehending Comprehension • I Found My Dad inside
My Book • Images in My Head

6. **Value the reading responses of young people.**   *85*
The Great Gatsby Fails English • Books and Biscotti • Has
Anyone Seen My Book Report?

7. **View writing as literacy.**   *93*
   Writing: The Other Side of the Literacy Coin • The Unfriendly
   Letter • I Will Never Learn to Make a Capital "B"

8. **Recognize the ages and stages of individuals.**   *103*
   I Won't Read, So Don't Ask Me • The Invisible Non-Reader •
   Boys Will be Boys, and Girls Will Be Readers • Wrestling With
   Ideas

9. **Explore how words work.**   *115*
   Stick-handling through the Words • Parsing Our Way into
   Oblivion • The Phonics War • The Writing on the
   Living-Room Wall • Ms. Moffett Is Fragile Today • Does
   Spelling Count? • How Should We Teach Spelling? •
   Laughing All the Way to the Word Bank • Playing Our Way
   into Word Power

10. **Turn printed texts into active learning.**   *135*
    Variations on a Theme • The School Assembly • Reading the
    War

11. **Focus on literacy in every subject.**   *143*
    Don't Know Much about Biology • Project Pain • Adding
    and Subtracting Our Way to Literacy

12. **Welcome kids into the culture of literacy.**   *153*
    Only the Rich Can Read • What Does a Literacy Teacher Look
    Like? • Twenty-Two Things that Twenty-Two Boys Taught
    Me • Literacy Rituals and Ceremonies • There's a Parent
    Peering in the Window! • Looking in the Rear-View Mirror

101 Literacy Events   *173*

1. Expand our definition of literacy.

> Once upon a time there was a child,
> who was accompanied by an adult,
> and the adult had a book
> and the adult read.
> And the child, fascinated,
> listened to how oral language
> became written language.
>
> —Emilia Ferreiro

Dick and Jane Have Moved On

Dick and Jane still live in today's world, even though they have been retired from a reading series for half a century. Their white-bread neighbourhood, their simple, stereotyped lives, still seem to spark our sentimental memories of learning to read, even though most adults have never met them in books. Yet they are immortalized on fridge magnets and greeting cards, and even in satirical versions on TV. Such iconic power! Of course, there were many versions of Dick and Jane over the decades they lasted in schools, and they heralded the movement labelled "whole word" reading programs, giving fuel for fifty years to people who wanted to polarize teaching methodologies, often for their own interests.

We know that young children use every technique they can in their attempts at becoming readers: some can read "pterodactyl" before "and" or "but." And, of course, environmental print floods their daily lives, in fast-food restaurants, names on presents, labels on toys, titles in TV programs. And one pattern from a specific word can lead to an awareness of five others, so that young readers build up their automatic sight vocabularies as they make connections from one sequence of letters to the next.

The first word I can remember being challenged by was "Czar," since it was spelled two ways in the story—"Tsar" and "Czar." Emerging readers need lots of support in making sense of words, so that they are never faced with a text where each word has to be examined letter by letter, sounded out, tasted, and spat out. No one would read if that were the case. And, of course, some children don't. These non-readers were never able to lift the words off the page and into their literacy minds, to be used again in a different story. They needed someone to sit beside them and show them the secrets; they didn't need to be handcuffed and deprived of the wonderful feelings of accomplishment when those squiggles on the page revealed actual meaning. Years ago, educational activist John Holt said that schools should be full of senior citizens wearing badges that read, "Ask me!" They would help a child with any difficult word, without reprimand or shame. As adults—parents and teachers alike—we need to remember that the literacy journey never ends, and welcome each novice traveller, make them comfortable, and guide them through the territory, pointing out significant sights along the way, and revelling in the responses of the voyager. Our personal satisfaction comes not from the journey, but from seeing the pleasure and satisfaction on the faces of those we mentor. Literacy mentors like us are so fortunate, because we see the results of our work, day by day, word by word.

I began to teach reading in the 1960s, when Bill Martin, Jr., led us to the literacy cave with *Brown Bear, Brown Bear,* when Brian Way had us all join the circle and work together, when Sylvia Ashton-Warner found that the words that really mattered to new readers tapped into their hopes and fears and imaginations, when play time began to involve materials and tools used in daily life, and children hammered real nails with real hammers. It was so exciting to teach with stories written by authors, not typists, in which the children and the teacher could frame the author and the text within their own life experiences. In our lust for life connections, we began to note that the story between and beyond the lines might hold more fascination for the reader, that Baby Sally might sometimes throw up on Mother's shoes, that Dick might hate sports and love poetry, that Jane might have severe bouts of depression, that Father might take holidays by himself, and that Mother might have weight problems after giving birth to three children.

When we are allowed to grow alongside someone with expertise and knowledge, we are living in real time, apprentice and master.

I want to learn to read and write like you.
I need to learn to read and write like you.

Two memories come to mind.

In the first, I'm sitting beside my five-year-old nephew, Phillip, on the deck at the cottage, reading a novel, and watching him pretend to read one, seeing him turning a page every time I do, following my lead. What a natural way to enter reading!

In the second, I'm nailing a birdhouse to a pole in the yard, after my friend Jim and my son Jay have built it together in Jim's shop behind his house. Jay had drawn on, sawed, nailed, and painted real wood with real tools, guided by Master Jim.

This is a metaphor for how we learn to read; as apprentices, we sit alongside a master reader, and we listen and watch as the sound of the reader's voice turns the printed code into meaning that makes us laugh or wonder or question or know. We understand how birdhouses are built, just as we grasp the power of the printed code. Life's experiences build a reader's contextual knowledge bank, so as we meet texts in print or onscreen, we can connect to the thoughts and perceptions of the writer. We must bring our lives to the text in order to become meaning-makers, to become readers. That is how concrete experiences by hand can move us into virtual experiences by eye. Birds can teach us to read.

As someone said, a little hand can type the number 0 on a computer keyboard. But when the same little hand draws the number 0 freehand, the mind attached to it suddenly understands what roundness means. Everything matters. A poet said, "Only connect." For all of us, connecting things is the path to learning. How can we help students to connect to the text they are to work with, to imagine themselves into what the words mean and symbolize, rather than just staring at the squiggles? For me, the words must dissolve into the events they describe, or there is no reading. In a sense, words are the medium that will help us discover the messages they create. All print is written in invisible ink that requires the reader's heated passion in order to reveal the clues that can lead towards constructing meaning with it. We really can't blame Dick and Jane. But we can move on down the road to more significant story heroes, and then we're on our way to redefining the reading process: making sense of texts that matter to us, whether encoded in print, onscreen or voice, or a combination of them all.

Jean Little is one of our most celebrated authors of children's books. She is also blind. Once, after a conference, I drove her back to her hotel, where she asked the desk clerk if her parcel of new "talking books" had arrived. She said, "I can't go to sleep without reading a book."

Has Anything Really Changed?

About one-third of our population in North America lacks basic literacy skills to function successfully. We only need to look among the dropouts, the soaring prison populations or the homeless to find the most visible functionally illiterate, but there are many more invisible illiterates. There has been a decline in the readership of books and newspapers, especially of fiction, and the literary culture loses more young people every year, a retreat from complex and deeply structured modes of printed texts. How do we nurture in our young people a love and need for the printed word? How do we build a culture of literacy that is inclusive of the multitude of text forms, so that intensive and extensive experiences are part of the continuum of literacy? How can we enhance literacy, expand competency, with electronic texts? We need to rethink literacy and how we will support students.

In March 2006, the *New York Times* published a front-page article on the tendency of schools to push reading and math at the expense of all other subjects. At one high school in Sacramento, 150 students out of 850 spend five of their six class periods on math, reading, and gym, leaving only one period for all other subjects. Those students doing poorly are prohibited from taking any classes other than math, reading, and gym. This pressure comes from state test scores, and raising those scores is the single goal for many schools. What kind of citizens will emerge from this "basic" education is beyond me. But what interests me most is what these kids are reading. Are there no selections on any topics that might be connected to the rest of the curriculum? Are they mandated to read only one genre? Who are the authors who seem to speak to these students? What care is being taken to develop independent, thinking individuals? What do they do with what they have read? Are writing and technology inherent parts of the program? Are we causing these students to believe that this is what reading as adults will look like? Do we care?

One billion children (one in two children in the world) live in poverty, 640 million live without adequate shelter, 400 million have no access to safe water, and 270 million have no access to health services; 10.6 million died in 2003 before they reached the age of five, and 1 billion people, two-thirds of them women, are illiterate. Economically poor countries are having great difficulty overcoming illiteracy, with no provisions guaranteeing minimum schooling, and so-called wealthy countries are deeply concerned about the low levels of literacy among up to half of their populations. What do we mean by the term "functional literacy"? It is often used to describe individuals who are able to read simple forms of printed texts, who are not readers in the complete sense of the term, accurate, fluent, resourceful readers who gain pleasure and insight from reading, who take pleasure in reading, who choose to read different texts in daily life, who are able to browse through the range of different texts in a literate culture. Teachers at every level of schooling complain that many students can neither read nor write effectively, and remedial literacy classes are common right through to graduate programs at university, and, of course, in business. Graduation from a school system does not guarantee literacy success, even using the simplest definition of literacy competence: the ability to carry out basic tasks, such as filling out an employment application, completing a tax form, following written instructions, reading a newspaper, reading traffic signs, consulting a dictionary or understanding a bus schedule (and we haven't even included the world of technology).

Have there been changes in how we attempt to help youngsters move toward literacy? Of course, and it has often been painful and difficult. In a technological world, where two-year-olds are working at computers, the mode and content of literacy have altered. In my years of teaching, I have had to adapt my own behaviours, rethink policy and pedagogy, learn new techniques for making and interpreting print and image, re-examine cultural agendas, and continue to experience the world through what we can call "multi-literacies"—the page, computer screen, cellphone screen, television, etc. The one who knows the most facts about a topic is no longer the winner, except in the aptly named game of Trivial Pursuit. We need to seek out and interpret information, use all the facets of our intelligence to make the most sense of what we encounter, and move our quests into thoughtful and reflective knowledge. And what of emotions, ethics, morality, humanness? How do they affect our construct of the educated person? We interpret text through our own value system; just think of a book on religion, or a political opinion column in a newspaper. Literacy has never been devoted to only the honourable; unscrupulous people may be very literate. The Nazis read books; there are manuals for terrorists. Rather, we need to see literacy as a series of processes that can offer us a means, a pathway, to deeper, more complex understandings and constructions of our own worlds. The value of literacy education, both inside and outside schools, involves what we do with what we learn, and with whom we live.

The goals of education have changed since Charles Dickens attacked wicked schools in *Hard Times* (remember the headmaster, Mr. Gradgrind?), but there are constants: the values and the beliefs inherent in caring for the minds and spirits and lives of all young people resonate with Dickens's dreams.

The New Literacies

Our definitions of reading and reading instruction are changing. And how we see the world changes as a result. What are called the "new literacies" are profoundly shaping the ways in which we view and use language. Just as the telephone altered communication strategies, our children will encounter a wide and perhaps unthought-of variety of information and communication technologies. Just think of video cameras, web editors, spreadsheets, list serves, blogs, Power Point, virtual worlds, and dozens more. Our traditional way of thinking about and defining literacy will be insufficient if we hope to provide youngsters with what they will need to be full participants in the world of the future. As trade barriers fall and global trade expands, the workplace is altering. Within an organization, teams need to make important decisions as they identify problems, locate useful information, synthesize what they find, and communicate the solution to others in the company. These collaborative teams need new, more effective ways of working. Critical literacies and analytical skills will be requirements of workers. And politics relies heavily on new modes of literacy as representatives and campaign supporters for all parties organize online support communities. Therefore our youngsters will require technological expertise in their home, work, and civic lives. They will need to be plugged in for survival.

In 1998, Finland's Ministry of Education provided every teacher with five weeks of paid release time for professional development in the use and instruction of new informational technologies. All sixth-grade children have a portable telephone, but they don't just talk to each other; in fact, they use the keypad as a computer keyboard, and they communicate by typing messages—"texting" with each other. But the most interesting aspect of this information phenomenon is that futurists predict that in two years all seven-year-olds there will be involved in the same activity. Already (you may own one yourself), manufacturers have designed palm-sized devices to make the whole process simpler. And Finland—home of Nokia—leads the field in reading scores on international tests. (The country also boasts the highest library usage, the most newspapers read per capita, subtitles on TV programs for children, and a sense of community responsibility for literacy teaching.)

Does literacy presuppose print? Does literacy comprehension mean comprehension of only printed text, or comprehension of a message that has permanence? To celebrate Queen Elizabeth's eightieth birthday, all the newspapers in England distributed a free CD-Rom of Roald Dahl's children's novel *The Twits*. Is this a literacy event?

Print itself does not hold prominence over visuals, or combinations of both. While the literacy inherent in each mode involves composition, decoding comprehension, and response, changes in how text forms function will alter or expand our definition of literacy. Think of the multimedia in a website: as the mouse clicks, meaning-bearing icons, animations, and video clips may appear, along with graphics of all types, pop-ups, an entire sign system dependent upon the "reader's" tool kit. Isn't it paradoxical that as we invent universal symbol systems, we also find a growing diversity of cultures and languages with all the nations and groups involved? We will need to help readers develop multiple perspectives if they are to successfully communicate in their wide-ranging, plugged-in world.

But we know that the traditional foundations of literacy are the building blocks: word and vocabulary recognition, decoding knowledge, comprehension, critical analysis, the writing process, and spelling are all requirements. Yet the new literacies will demand other skills, new competencies, in order for people to function as literate citizens. And, of course, speed has become an adjunct literacy tool with computers. This means that limited readers will need help learning to skim websites containing enormous amounts of information, to link web pages, and to evaluate text in all its forms. How can we best assist them in becoming modern, competent literacy participants?

Literacy changes as society demands it change. Who we are will depend on the world we live in, and how we are expected to function. McLuhan was right: The medium is the message in so many ways.

We can think of four basic literacy divisions:

- school literacy (measured by assessment)
- life literacy (cultural, workplace, and recreational literacy)
- print literacy (literature, non-fiction, popular media)
- technological literacy (computer and internet images and words in combination)

If teachers do not prepare students for the literacies required in their future lives, what should they be teaching? Business spends millions of dollars training employees in the literacies required for effective practice, and this will continue as changes occur in the needs of the workplace.

I am worried about inequity within different schools. While some students spend hours reading required texts, others enjoy different types of texts, including technology, participating in inquiries that involve intensive and extensive opportunities for interpreting ideas. What literacy strengths do students leave school with? What impressions do they have of the functions of literacy in their lives? Attitudes towards literacy may determine the level of engagement students will seek with the text forms they encounter. The way we incorporate texts into our schools' curricula can lead to limitations in the lives of the students. In today's world, literacy is more than the ability to sign one's name. Social and work considerations present severe challenges to youngsters with strong literacy deficits. But now we have added to the difficulties of reading manuals, newspapers, and novels the immensity of the functions of the internet and its permutations and combinations.

But we have found that while computers eliminate problems with cursive writing, left-handedness, and copying out revised versions, they do not ameliorate the cognitive processes of learning to read and write. Bill Gates has said that the only prerequisite for computer success is literacy.

We only need to think about different readers' responses to a newspaper article, a political speech, a new CD, a religious film or a novel to realize that print requires interpretation if meaning is to be created. The reader's encounter with a printed work is complex, determined by the life experiences of the reader as he or she negotiates the relationship between the ideas of the writer and the reader's experiences. Meaning-making with text is a dynamic interaction, depending as well upon the format and the context of the text. Many county fairs in the US are updating activities, with contests for decorated skateboards and text messaging, and a "cellfest" including videos and photos created on cellphones.

Linguistic and cultural differences offer us a wealth of opportunities, an enrichment of possibilities. Literacy is a foundation of citizenry in any language, a right of freedom. As we recognize the complexities of society's issues, we see the need for "reading" at the deepest level, for recognizing the shades of grey between black-and-white extremes. Are those who read only minimal text in any form or format susceptible to control by corporations, unethical political leaders or charlatans? An informed citizenry requires competency in different text forms.

In many countries, reading doesn't mean what it did two or three centuries ago. There are new ways of representing ideas, new ways of encoding language, new ways of how we spend time reading and writing. Those of us who grew up without computers will never have the ease of children born inside the technological revolution. It takes time for us as teachers or parents to understand and accept change, and to act as participants in the new environment. We fear the end of a book culture, of the icon that has represented wisdom in our world. We're afraid someone has struck the delete key, and all this while we're watching television in the living room as the children watch their own programs in their bedrooms.

If You Don't Read Now, You Can't Watch TV Tonight!

So many parents ask me, often with tears in their eyes, why their children don't choose to read books, even though they have been read to all through childhood, even though they have been surrounded by books, and even though their parents find great satisfaction and comfort in their companionship with books. Working with the new definition of literacy helps me open their minds to what a child may be reading, and often that includes many different types of texts—just not what parents would wish. Computers, television, radio, songs, newspapers, comics, graphic novels, magazines, TV guides, game manuals, sports statistics, subject course books, homework, school novels, after-school play rehearsals, music practice; and the list goes on. (Did I forget to mention tests, or exams, or assignments that require children to answer forty questions about a novel that held no romance for them or their teachers?) Yet it is cold comfort for those parents who fondly imagine the adolescent in his bed, late in the evening, flashlight in hand, devouring a novel so well crafted, so magical, that the reading cuts into the night of intended sleep, and rather than shout, "Lights off!" they smile at the dream child and quietly leave him to fall asleep with the book still in his hands. Too often parents remember the family ritual of bedtime reading, when parent and child became one, fused by the power of a story, escaping loneliness for the child and separation for the adult. The weight of job and housework and finances disappeared as the pages were turned, and the child's literacy experiences depended upon the master reader, who sat beside her, warming the bed and the night and the soul.

But why for a moment believe those bedtime moments aren't to be valued and treasured? Of course children have always learned from sharing books and stories with someone who loved them—the language, the patterns, the moral implications, the themes, the issues, the characters, the modelling by a literate, wise adult. Treasure those times, just as you remember the board games you played together at the cottage, the paintings you put on the fridge, the cold nights in the hockey arena. We didn't read books to our children for future training; we read because of a childhood imperative. We shared stories to be a part of life together.

Did we ever betray the bond between reader and listener? Did we ever ask those dreaded comprehension questions of the picture book we had just marvelled at? Once, after reading my son "Snow White," I tried playing a game with him, and suggested that we role-play the wicked queen and Snow White. And when I asked him as Snow White if she would like a nice ripe pear from my basket, he said, "That's not how it goes," and his voice was tinged with fear. The sharing time was finished. So many children now wait for the other shoe to drop after hearing a story; they know that there must be more to this apple than the great bitter-sweet taste it leaves on the tongue. Keep reading to the children, I shout. One of my friends read to his kids every night into the teenage years, not so they would buy books, but so they would hear stories and find their imaginations, besotted with words they never would have met but for the writers and artists who create literary dreams.

We can only make people read what they don't want to read as long as they are in school. So many parents have spoken to me about their son (or daughter) who they feel no longer chooses to read. But when I question them about their child's reading behaviours, their attitude shifts quite quickly. All I have to say is "What don't they read?" and the answer is always the same: novels. We still judge the literacy worth of individuals by this one particular art form's place in their lives. All of a sudden, when parents begin listing the various modes of print that fill up their child's life, they remember that of course he reads—computers, sports pages, comics, game manuals, TV guides, school textbooks; the list goes on and on. Some teachers and parents are relieved by this recognition of what they secretly knew. I often receive emails from parents the day after meeting them, thanking me for helping them to paint a larger picture of their children's literacy lives than the narrow one prevalent in our society, especially in schools.

Never fear: print texts will fill their lives again, alongside their music and their videos, perhaps integrated with visuals and sound, on small, hand-held computers. But we have shaped books in different fashions for centuries, and we will continue to do so. However, what we decide to say, to construct, to create, may depend on the experiences our children encounter in their times with us. It's such a big responsibility for parents and teachers that sometimes it's easier to blame the kids.

But those of us who spend our leisure time among books want to pass on our love of this practice; we want others to join us in the book club, to enter a bookstore or a library with our excitement, and to leave fulfilled even before we read our selections with the expectations that lie within. We read the reviews, wait for the Saturday newspaper section devoted to books, talk to our colleagues about book gossip, and hoard our new purchases for holiday reading. And unhappily, we sometimes resort to punishing those youngsters who choose not to read what we loved; we rail against their hopeless literacy future, and we drive a wedge with our books between the children and our love for them. Books as crass weapons of destruction. Books as chores, like taking out the garbage.

There must be a better way. Can we reconcile children and books as they grow into adulthood? We can; we do with many. It means we will have to rethink our goals, our values, our paralyzing ability to shame and humiliate a novice reader, our disdain for lesser writers, our need to be seen as *au courant* with the latest and the critically acclaimed. We will have to see texts as filling the world, so that we can select those few that will change us, fulfill us, surprise us, validate us, and connect us to our families, friends, and fellow citizens. Some will be print, some image, some both, most electronic, a few on papyrus or pulp. Every child whispers: "Help me to be able to make meaning with the texts I want or need to read, and I'll be grateful."

But now the television in his room is playing, his one or two hours of homework are complete, and the new issue of his music magazine is open. His life is full of other texts, other dreams. The new century means a new approach to literacy, to text, and to making meaning. In the last century we invented the adolescent, just as the Victorians invented childhood. We may buy them *The Call of the Wild*, but they will respond to the call of the mall. The number of inventions that will be marketed to our youth will continue to multiply every year, and the content of life will keep exploding. As with a closet jammed with too much of everything, some things will have to be omitted, thrown away, cast aside. This is especially true in school, where we teachers cling to what we know, even to what we experienced as children or as students ourselves. We do not escape the contemporary world by hiding inside our brick buildings, but sometimes our curricula do, along with our resources. Schools as repositories for old books, old memories.

Who Can Read?

Why are so many of our students unable to read, according to so many news reports? What are their chances for developing literacy competencies or interest in or enthusiasm for reading?

19

We know that each child in North America spends an average of four hours a day in front of a TV. The images of cartoons, commercials, videos, and sensational action programs wash over the child daily. This constant stimulation and effortless absorption without much interpretation or reflection is complex competition for the humble—and sometimes complicated—book.

Like most people, I value and need media experiences, but I wonder how many children will meet books, to discover the options they can bring to their choices in life. For those without opportunities to discuss books in their homes, schools can provide a balance to the multitude of literacies children will find valuable in their lives. But what will those book experiences be composed of? Required textbooks, with carefully regulated and simplified language; worksheets and test items. And what of selection, of learning how to choose from the quantity of materials those resources that will be significant to the young reader? Many of us rely on media – reviews, advertisements, popular talk shows—for our book choices. Next year will see the launch of the Sony Reader, a portable device for digital books and documents, along with digitized titles from major publishers. The Reader is the size of a thin paperback and weighs 250 grams. Writing in the *New York Times*, Kevin Kelly of *Wired* magazine creates a fascinating manifesto for the change that's coming with our definition of books. "The world's texts are being electronically copied, digitized, searched and linked." The force of the web lies in the power of relationships. Search engines create a trillion electronic connections through the web.

Once text (any text) is digital, books seep out of their bindings and weave themselves together. The collective intelligence of a library allows us to see things we can't see in a single, isolated book. The universal library becomes one very, very, very large single text: the world's only book, a single, liquid fabric of inter-connected words and ideas.

Fortunately, books and screens will co-exist for the near future. Book people are strong-willed proponents of the paper-print media, and technology will continue to expand as young people are born wireless.

But children will need parents, teachers, librarians, and friends to promote and provide choices to extend and enrich their literacy options with different texts, along with time and places and opportunities for adding new ones to their crowded lives.

Remember how it felt as a young child to sit beside someone who cared about you and read aloud to you. As you heard the words, you saw the world being created in your imagination. And the illustrations and images pulled you even further into this book experience, until you wanted to be in control of your own story-making, translating the text symbols into spoken language, breaking the code, finding the wonder inside the words.

I like what the noted literacy authority Emilia Ferreiro says about learning to read:

> The relation between graphic markings and language is at the beginning a magical one that sets up a triad: an interpretation, a child, and a set of marks. The interpretation informs the child that these markings have special powers: just by looking at them language is produced. What is it in these markings that causes the eye to make the mouth produce language? The reader seems to speak for the other there present, but what he says are not his own words, rather the words of an "other" who can multiply into many "others" that emerge from who knows where, hidden as well behind those marks. The reader speaks, but is not he who speaks; the reader says, but what is said is not his own saying, rather that of ghosts who become real through his voice.

Is there time for printed text in the lives of today's children? Even children in daycare view TV and videos, and very young children are on good terms with Baby Einstein media. There are televisions in every room of many houses, including bedrooms (switched on during breakfast, lunch, and dinner), computers, cellphones, iPods, and video games drawing children in. How much modelling of book reading do they see in their parents' own literacy lives of magazines, newspapers, DVDs, and CDs? Parents seem to find time to drive to the video/DVD store at least once a week, passing by at least one library or bookstore on their way. I say this as a TV viewer, a reader of two newspapers a day and three or four magazines a week, a driver with a dashboard crammed with CDs, and a reader of many types of books, for children, teens, and adults. Of course, time for reading books has diminished in my life as other opportunities have filled my days. But as literacy mentors for children, we are required to live alongside our expectations for children. As adults, do we make time for reading a variety of text forms? Do we let children see us as book-aware, reading aloud to them at different times in the day, clipping a newspaper column, commenting on a magazine article, sharing book news with a friend, buying books as gifts, participating in a book club, placing books in central positions in our homes, going to the library, finding lists of new and suitable books for youngsters? How will we develop in our children a passion for reading different texts, so that their complex futures can be full of paths toward information, knowledge, and wisdom? And I would add joy and satisfaction.

Reading in the Air

Because of my work in education, I fly a great deal on my way to speak to groups of teachers and parents, and I have a habit of reading a variety of texts in flight, since I value this time away from duty, the phone, etc. For example, on a flight from

Toronto to Los Angeles, I can read two magazines, a novel, and preview several children's picture books. There are some passengers who laugh at a grown man reading a picture book on an airplane, but literacy is part of my life wherever I am. Squeezed between two businessmen, I hold my book aloft in my right hand, pictures facing the seat ahead, as I do in all the classrooms I visit, for I have developed amazing peripheral vision, and I now need to read everything in this fashion. And I read out loud, but no amount of persuasion will cause the two guys beside me to join in. Once I brought along a pop-up book, but that did cause anxiety among the male passengers when I asked them what they thought might pop up next.

I can't understand what people think they are going to do on a four-hour flight without reading materials. Time and again the person next to me begins a frantic search for something to read, even grasping at the message on the sick bag. What have we done to make the act of reading so foreign in our culture? A steward on one flight, noticing that I had been reading for a while, commented, "You must be an author, since you seem to enjoy books so much." On a flight to Colorado, three young men in their late teens were sitting across from me on their first parentless ski trip, with, of course, nothing to read. As I was having fun with my children's books, I could see the guilt on their faces, and they all picked up that meaningless magazine you get for free on all airplanes that is seldom worth reading, and they held their copies up, pretending to read like children in a kindergarten class. As is my habit, I leaned over and said, "Didn't your moms pack any books or magazines with your underwear?" There was no response, but I wonder about a society that purchases designer briefs for their children no matter what the cost, with little or no thought about clothing their minds.

Of course, we now have iPods and personal DVD players and computer games to fill the time, but I still carry my paper texts on board, hoping for some peaceful time in relative silence. A reading dinosaur.

On one flight, I found myself sitting between two young people who were both reading hardcover books. I could see that they had both chosen library books for this journey. Such a feeling of hope welled up in me. Hurray for the library habit that some adults had instilled in these two now literate people. I do see others reading on airplanes, always in first class, sometimes in the economy seats in which I sit. More and more travellers are using laptop computers to finish office work, but I'm always staring and hoping. On a trip I took last year, a young boy across from me wearing a yarmulke never took his eyes from his religious book. Once, in New York, the airport was fogged in, and I was forced to wait three hours for my plane. In the waiting room, I found myself surrounded by about twenty young men, all wearing Armani suits, and eventually discovered they were the New York Islanders hockey team. I like to ask teachers at conferences what they think the players were doing during the delay, and they invariably tell me that they were girl-watching, playing video games, drinking, and so on. But when I ask eighth-graders the same question, they tell me that they were probably reading, and of course, the kids are right. What a variety of print resources, from novels to magazines, from the stock market to newspapers! One player was reading aloud from an article in the paper describing last night's game to his reading group, who were responding appropriately with great guffaws.

People from all walks of life do read, and young people need to see this role-modelling. We have all read of or been part of projects in which a whole school reads silently for twenty minutes, including the children, the teachers, the principal, the secretary, the caretaker, but these motivating schemes can only be successful if the participants value the program, and if their reading presents to the students a picture of adults engaged with print because they value the process. I once overheard a phys-ed instructor telling his charges that it wasn't his idea that they had to read and waste their game time; he certainly wasn't helping achieve the goal of demonstrating the value of literacy. There are better ways that teachers have found for promoting school-wide literacy, where adults share their reading behaviours in moving and involving ways. And the second factor for success is that the students do something with what they have read: as the saying goes, "It takes two to read a book." We need to think about what we have read by interacting with others, for we only know what we think when we try to articulate our thoughts. That is why school can be such a powerful force in teaching literacy; we have a built-in community for exploring our print-generated ideas.

Sitting in the airport during a two-hour delay, I watched the reading behaviours of the passengers, especially the youngsters. A girl eleven or twelve years of age, sporting a bared midriff and carefully streaked hair, was having her younger sister, aged seven or eight, read aloud to her from a paperback chapter book, correcting her pronunciation errors, unconcerned with any meaning-making on her sibling's part. She herself, after listening to a few pages, began to read an Agatha Christie murder mystery. (Is this how those with no teaching background think youngsters learn to read? How would those of us with professional training handle a similar situation?)

A young boy with a very responsive and caring mother read silently, asking his older brother for help when a difficult word arose. (Does strong parenting give us the ability to persevere, requiring support only when we decide it is needed?)

A gum-chewing boy in senior high was sitting beside his older brother, who spotted a textbook in his brother's bag. Lifting it out, he began to skim it back to front, pausing when an item appeared significant. His brother stared at him for ten minutes, and finally asked, "Why are you reading a textbook?"

"Some neat stuff in here," the older brother replied. "I always read my schoolbooks cover to cover before we start to use them. Makes it easier." (How can two siblings have such different attitudes towards reading?)

On the airplane, the youngster in the seat beside me read a Harry Potter novel for the entire flight, never looking up except to take a glass of soda pop. I asked him how the book was, and he said, "As good as all the others." (What causes a literary fad to take over, and how can we celebrate literature and jump on the bandwagon without writing manuals and co-opting what the children need to hold in their own subculture?)

And why are so many in *business class* reading? Is it a prerequisite of wealth? Of education? Of power?

Too many people equate literacy with having to read and be examined on what other people choose, and our pop culture seems to reinforce this sad misconception. Imagine a beer commercial in which five guys in jogging attire are sitting on the porch in the early evening, and one says to the others, "Hey, let's grab some brews and go read." It's not going to happen.

My son used to love playing basketball on Saturday mornings, which necessitated my driving him to and from the arena. While I constantly complained about the driving, one benefit was that I could read in the bleachers during the hour of practice. However, one of the coaches noticed me and commented, "Some of the fathers come an hour early and play before the kids do. That might help you get in shape."

I said that I would be pleased to come an hour earlier and moderate a book club, because I felt those coaches might gain some brain. But we were at an impasse. The coaches volunteered their time for my son and I will always be grateful, but I wish there were places where fathers and sons could voluntarily gather to celebrate the written word on Saturday mornings. (A friend once said he knew of such a place: the temple service at his synagogue.)

Hockey was easier. The driving was the same, but the practices and the games were in the late evening, and no one seemed to notice those few of us in the last rows, reading away in the cold, sipping hot chocolate. The "us" included several fathers who had banded together in an informal reading club while our well-armed sons fought the good ice fight down below. Perhaps for the first time in my life, I welcomed and felt part of the strange phenomenon called sport.

What constitutes literacy has changed throughout history. It has only recently become expected and desirable to be fully literate in every format and genre, and demeaning not to be so.

Children today are born into the age of television and computer screens, but the image has not replaced the alphabetical code. We continue to read and write text. The page form is being replaced by text that rolls vertically, with forms of email and text messages that are multi-modal in nature as our relationship with printed text alters and mutates. We now see a multitude of ways of recording thoughts and feelings for others to "read" and interpret.

We support kindergarten and other primary students in writing down their thoughts and feelings, without fear of not knowing all of the conventions of print. We celebrate their efforts at writing with markers and pencils and crayons and we understand what they are trying to say. Nor are they limited to only stories; they write lists, and descriptions, and they read everything from poems to labels. They are constructing text. They are beginning literacy practices of browsing among different text types and genres that will continue all their lives. New technologies are teaching us that there are multi-literacies involving different modes of representing thought.

A future literate culture will be determined not only by its literature—fiction or non-fiction—but also by newspapers, magazines, television, computers, networks, films, CD-Roms, hypertext, email, and other forms yet to be created.

2. Include comics, magazines, songs, poems, manuals, and novels as part of reading.

How Comic Books Defeated School

When I was in seventh grade, comic books were my main source of literacy delight. I collected dozens if not hundreds of them and traded them with friends every Friday evening after dinner. The memory of sitting in the backseat of our old car in the driveway, in my private cocoon, eating apples picked from a tree in the ravine, and reading five new comic books, still warms my aging heart. My father read my comics when I was finished with them, and it didn't matter how teachers felt about them; in fact, the taboo factor worked in their favour as a popular icon of childhood. For a time in the early fifties, comic books were printed in only black-and-white—all the colour had been removed in the hope of dissuading young readers. But after a brief few months, Superman's tights were blue again. Of course, with the hundreds of thousands of volumes of Manga printed today in black-and-white, with male readers numbering in the millions, and the rise in popularity of graphic novels, publishers are working night and day to meet the demands of youngsters and of teachers and librarians who have accepted the literary tastes of many boys in order to promote literacy growth. If they'll read it, we'll buy it.

At a talk I recently gave to educators, a teacher approached me at the end of the evening, and told me of his love of comic books, about his collection of first editions, his trip to the comic book convention where thousands of men with this hobby gathered to listen to writers, linguists, artists, illustrators, and sociologists discuss this misunderstood art form.

He said, "I've always hidden this part of my life from fellow teachers, but now I want to start a comic book club in my school and redeem this literature in the eyes of educators.'

Hurrah for courageous young teachers who want to explore a variety of texts with their students, and can we add powerful graphic novels to the mix, as well as action novels by some of the amazing writers for young people, so that his students will find options for literacy that they never thought existed.

The maxim "quantity before quality" has great validity when it comes to building fluent readers. As they pore over new issues of favourite comic books, kids find the words alongside the visuals, sometimes inside the pictures, or as running text along the bottom of the page, or in dialogue balloons that somehow pull the reader into engaging with and interpreting the multi-modal text. This reminds me of how complicated films that require subtitles seem to us when we are tired or in need of losing ourselves to the screen images that wash over us. At a recent movie where future ads for films were shown before the feature, the young man in front of me cried out: "Whoa, a thinking film! We aren't going to that one." I want to add "Yet." I have some sympathy, but at this stage in my life, I yearn for films from other countries, other cultures, films that lift me from my present life. I search out subtitled films, but I recognize their complications and the contexts necessary for this dual medium of text and images to work effectively. Still, *The Passion of the Christ*, which was mainly in Aramaic with subtitles, drew millions of ticket purchasers to cinemas all over the world, and no one seemed put off by the print they read at the same time as they "read" the images. We bring our own needs to every experience with text, whether those in charge want us to or not.

At a sleepover at my friend Robert's house when I was ten or eleven, I was shocked to find him reading a hardcover collection of animal stories by Ernest Thompson Seton, while I devoured two new comics I had brought with me. I did experience a pang of guilt: Is this what well-brought up boys read in the evening? Am I betraying my working-class background, embarrassing my parents, ruining my future job prospects? I remember this fifty years later. Comic books will always have that rough edge about them, literature that is smudged by our need for the critically acclaimed canon, as we struggle to balance our cultural call with children's populist needs.

I have now read all of Seton's stories of foxes and wolves and badgers. I have even included one or two in each student anthology that I have put together over the years. Everything in its place, I suppose. But should that place be the classroom? How do we open up options in texts if we value only what kids would choose to read without us? Do we matter? Is it an either/or question or are the different texts of our lives part of how and who we become? So many students see required reading as a necessary evil of school culture. They seldom revisit those high-school novels we hold in such high esteem.

Did Wonder Woman date? Menstruate? Or was she a drag queen? For me, it didn't matter. The game was action, male or female, and—*Pow! Bam!*—I was inside the text, on the roller coaster, moving through the story at the speed of light. I do think that racing through stacks of comics can promote X-ray visions, where we as readers see right though the print squiggle to the meaning, always striving to understand as we turn the pages faster and faster.

I must confess that I am addicted to *The New Yorker*. For Christmas one year, my son gave me the complete anthology of

31

fifty years of cartoons from the magazine. I actually remember most of them from the original issues. You can read a cartoon text (words and visuals), often in a second or two, and still remember it decades later. The cartoonist captures you in a moment in time, and never lets go. "Peanuts" cartoons gave me happiness at breakfast for decades – more than happiness; sometimes angst, as when Peppermint Patty told her friend Marcia about not having a mother. How can four frames signify so much? Of course, it's the accumulation of the frames over the years that adds the texture, the nuance, to my meaning-making, but Charles Schultz touches my soul again and again. Today, "Zits" and "Get Fuzzy" draw me into my morning paper. Words and pictures – I need them both, together; narrative encapsulated in one to four frames. I loved visiting my grandmother in Florida because the newspaper there had four whole pages of cartoons. Sometimes, reading the text itself doesn't even matter – we need to just read the pictures. Such is the power of the image.

Many of today's young readers enjoy reading a different type of book from those we are most familiar with: the graphic novel. This shouldn't come as a surprise in a world where visuals from television, videos, games, and computers fill so much of our youngsters' time. In an increasingly image-filled culture, this new literacy medium offers alternatives to traditional texts used in schools, while at the same time promoting literacy development. For many of us, comic books are tainted as a lesser genre, relegated to childhood's Saturday morning leisure time. But many of today's graphic novels include a complex, art-filled variety of genres, from fiction to biography, social studies, and science, covering social, economic, and political topics and themes that readers might not choose in other types of texts. As well, they present opportunities for incorporating media literacy into a school reading program, as students critically examine this word-and-image medium itself. Because of the apparent similarity between the comics and graphic novels they are often confused with one another. Graphic novels are extended narratives told in words and images. They are the most popular "novels" read by boys today. Comics are evolving as well. In a recent article in the *New York Times,* we learn that the new generation of comic superheroes will have the usual variety of special powers, but the faces behind the masks will represent black, Asian, and Hispanic crime fighters, who will inhabit "an alternate world that nevertheless reflects North American society."

The new literacies, as they have been labelled, are concerned with multi-modal texts, such as comics, magazines, newspapers, the internet, email, graphics, video, and sound. Together, these "texts" fill the lives of our students, and meaning accrues as students combine the messages from the different media into their own construct of the world.

We adults need to acknowledge our children's literacy lives with comics and graphic novels, admit to our own addiction if we have one, recognize the opportunities for incorporating comics and cartoons wherever possible, and open their young lives to all of the different texts they will want and need in their immediate and future lives. Turning up our noses at what children value has never led them toward wider choices as readers of texts. Keep those value judgments to yourself and recognize what they are. As a teaching friend of mine said: "Do you really want a ten-year-old boy to have the same literary tastes as a forty-year-old divorced teacher?" Never.

Literacy vs. Literature

I have spent most of my life in schools as a language arts teacher, and the lens through which I have observed most learning has focused on books for young people. I have worked with children, teachers, and parents for decades, attempting to persuade them that a curriculum full of worthwhile books is one of hope for enriching young people's lives. But with the recent findings and information on the new literacies, I am changing my views on what matters most: I want each reader to be able to read whatever texts he or she wants to or has to read, and to approach each text confidently, critically, and with any luck appreciatively.

I am saddened by the reading orphans, those people who are loath or hesitant to attempt to read any printed text. What happened to them? They never entered our circle, where we read anything and everything in front of us. They back away, shy away, from texts they would find interesting, even fascinating, if they could permit themselves the literacy experience. It seems that teacher indifference, teaching confusion or misguided pedagogy has resulted in this army of disbelievers, those who think that reading print is never worth it. What so many of us take for granted, they see as unsatisfying, even painful. Even the thought of reading texts, facing a book puts their stomachs in knots. That's why I have altered the direction of my professional life, and have moved to literacy education instead of literature courses. Literacy is the process of constructing and interpreting meaning with the text (print or visual) you need or want to experience. Literature is the text you read. And often literature connotes art, the canon, the best of cultural offerings. However, my interest lies in mentoring young readers, assisting them with the techniques of their apprenticeship in reading and writing. Of course I will use the best texts I can find; of course I will want to share the most significant texts society has to offer at a child's particular stage of growth; but these texts will include all types of modes of literacy – from nursery rhymes to computer manuals to Shakespeare to recipes to jokes and riddles. When I mention Danielle Steele, audiences of teachers usually groan; but millions of copies of her books have been sold and shared, and some of the audience members have copies in their handbags. I have had two men report to me via email that they have read novels by Ms. Steele. One confessed that, at the age of twelve, he sneaked into his sister's room and read a Steele novel, admitting that he was "shocked." The other was a seventy-two-year-old school trustee who explained that he read "everything" his wife brought home from the library. Get off their backs! Let them read what they choose to read. Offer other options if you can, but suspend judgment. Model what you value, shame no one. Text choice is personal.

Each year of my son's secondary schooling, I would ask his English teacher if the class would be reading a Canadian novel, play or poem. It never happened. That's not to say it doesn't in other classrooms, in other schools, but it didn't at Jay's. But then, how do we choose the resources we will incorporate into our programs? So many factors come into play! What do we find when we look in the Book Room? In the classroom to which we have been assigned? At district headquarters? Are we let in on the secrets of the budget, on the teams that determine purchases? Do consultants use our school for field testing, offering us pilot projects? Do we spend our own dollars and rack up credit card bills? All of the above, if you are active in literacy teaching. When I take new books to a conference talk, I am swamped by teachers busily writing down the names of every resource. When I mention a book in a talk, booksellers' shelves are emptied of that title at the break. Of course, these stories include novels, poems, and non-fiction written by those who create the artifacts of educated childhood. But we need to include the math texts, the basal readers, the spellers as well. Are you choosing, or just using, them?

I am old enough to remember when there was no choice. Arriving at school on my first day as a teacher, just fifteen minutes before school was to begin (I had worked in a grocery store, and it took just a minute to put on my apron), I found my classroom bereft of all books and resources, picked clean by the teachers who had been there for three weeks, papering their bulletin boards. I panicked and knocked on the door across the hall. The teacher answered and said, "You're late!" And that was that! This is decades ago, before teacher mentoring. Next, I paid a visit to the principal, who was too busy to help, but luckily I met the caretaker, who told me of hundreds of books down in the boiler room. The kids and I went on our first class excursion down to the basement, and returned with about 100 books for our classroom library. But when I began to distribute them, I realized that no two were the same, so on the spot I invented "individualized reading." How simple literacy teaching was a half a century ago! "Children, read!" Those who could did, and those who couldn't quit school. Now I want to go back and help them all into literacy. But the deed is done.

It is certainly impossible to read fiction without imagination, without placing yourself in a created world, conjuring up in your mind a different life, identifying strongly with a character and making all sorts of connections. The fictional lives are painted with the reader's imagination, just as the author has constructed a cosmos for the reader to attempt to understand and interpret. This is the imaginative negotiation between reader and author that comprises an act of fiction: and of course it is so difficult to measure imaginative development, so on the whole we don't try. And what we don't measure often disappears in a busy schedule, resulting in many readers who haven't experienced imaginative connections, who can't infer or empathize or connect – literal readers who never find gold in them thar books.

Are there times in the day, built into the classroom program, when children are permitted and encouraged to express thoughts and feelings through the arts, to wonder aloud in conversation about a significant text, to hypothesize about a science project they are about to begin, to risk attempting to problem-solve a complex math problem that may require several attempts? Are they allowed to try and try again without feeling failure but instead challenging their own puzzlements with imaginative efforts?

We seldom think of reading as an imaginative process, and the same could be said of our approach to writing. But the potential is there, whenever we decide that supporting and strengthening imagination is a vital ingredient of the literary processes. If we include ourselves as imaginative participants in the life of the classroom, then we can more easily notice and interpret the acts of imagination that enrich and extend everyone's learning.

Karen Gallas, in her fine book *Imagination and Literacy*, writes that "education is a process of working to master or acquire different discourses at increasing levels of complexity, and that full literacy implies an ability to work with all kinds of texts, especially those that seem unfamiliar. To be open to what a text offers depends on the action of the imagination." I can't find a better, more inclusive definition of reading in my own research. Everyone, including every child, reads each text he or she confronts based on life experiences, content and context, the type of discourse, the format, the style. The more I know about a topic, the more complex and sophisticated the texts I can manage. In this sense, reading success with a particular text is dependent on quantity and quality of previous exposure to similar texts. Let children read more, have more situations in which they can read, do more with what they read that really matters. Help them move along the curriculum of texts so that they can face and handle more complex texts, mentor them through conferences and conversations so that they are stretching their minds and their imaginations, cross-referencing their experiences of the text with those they have lived through.

Remember that many males stop reading fiction voluntarily at around twelve or thirteen years of age. However, they are often reading texts that schools may ignore completely. We seem to have put total faith in the novel, the most foreign, to many, of all print texts. Many males find it a very, very difficult medium. The research I have read indicates clearly that for many men, novels would not be their first choice of reading materials, and for those who choose this genre, we can look at the shelves of any large bookstore to see which types of novels are being purchased. Should we redress this situation, accept it or examine it as a cultural phenomenon?

Many people are confused about the difference between literature and literacy. The first definition of literature in the *Canadian Oxford Dictionary* is "written works, esp. those whose value lies in beauty of language or emotional effect." Too many parents and teachers regard only novels, poetry, and so-called literary non-fiction as literature. We have made many boys and men think that they are not readers because they don't happen to choose one of those genres. They may choose to read other kinds of texts, from *The New Yorker* to *Sports Illustrated*, both of which include the work of very fine writers, And, of course, many novels are not necessarily worth reading. The thinking of some that "novel" is the magic word for literacy is unfortunate for many readers. Today, even in grades three, four, and five, we see the whole-class novel as the main reading strategy. At least a third to half of a class often can't handle that text. Yet it is mandatory methodology, chapter by chapter. What is the goal? Is it literacy or literature? How we can have both is the question that needs to be examined.

Instead of teaching one book such as *To Kill a Mockingbird*, another thought might be to have thirty novels, some by black authors, which we read and share, and allow those perspectives to confront our own perspectives. We can look back at that novel or film and try to come to grips with the world in which it was written, when these writers lived, and how they are perceived by us. What an enriching event that would be, rather than having a chapter-by-chapter dissection led by the teacher.

I don't want to be "anti" any particular book, but rather "pro" the process of how we are going to explore it and make it part of the construct of our world.

We need to move towards supporting readers' decisions about the print resources they select—their newspapers, novels, magazines, their work and organizational materials, and what they read for fun and games. As with films and television, appreciating literature is a lifelong process, dependent on many factors, especially on readers' attitudes towards texts, often determined by their school experiences. What we need to consider in our teaching is how to increase the options that print resources can offer, and explore with students how different texts work—what to look for and what to expect—so that they can be informed about the choices they make and select the resources that will give them the most satisfaction.

How can we support youngsters who are reluctant readers to read what educators have labelled literature? As book lovers, we have all experienced the disappointment that comes when a child reveals his or her boredom with what we had felt was a significant piece of literature. Finding appropriate and interesting books for our students is a complicated task, but it is at the centre of our struggle to help them become appreciative readers, intent on extending their own knowledge. Backgrounds and abilities differ widely in the young people we meet, and yet we need to help each of them to begin to consider their responses to different texts, to reflect on why they feel as they do, and to consider the author's role in determining how they respond to the ideas and words in texts. Not surprisingly, reading the texts we want or need to read, in search of deeper understanding, may be the answer to many of the common problems teachers and parents face in promoting books to their young people.

Many parents want their children to read the classics. Many readers still enjoy them today, but as reading tastes and writing styles change, readers may make alternative choices. Students can find in the classics a different life from their own in language, custom, place, time or circumstance; for some, the differences can make the reading difficult. Independent readers may relish the depth of language and content that characterizes classics. And sometimes the media re-popularize old books, breathing new life into them, as we have seen with *Lord of the Rings.*

The literature canon for youngsters has not altered much over the last thirty or forty years. The same novels are used throughout most school districts in North America, without much awareness of equity or gender issues, or whether young people are being prepared for a life of literacy. *Catcher in the Rye, To Kill a Mockingbird, Lord of the Flies,* and *A Separate Peace* appear on virtually every class booklist at some point. They are often read and analyzed chapter by chapter, with too little attention paid to the impact of choice and the teaching strategy on the future literacy lives of the students. But reluctant readers tell us they want action, raw humour, familiarity, and complex illustrations; in contrast, teachers prefer elegance of story structure, sophistication of character development, complexity of description, irony, and references to other literature.

Young people are inundated with so many texts from television, cereal boxes, advertising, and computer games. How can a text medium full of long, uninterrupted print passages compete with the visual and aural sensations that beat upon them and catch them in what educator Ron Jobe has called the "web of immediacy"? Can we use the range of powerful literature we have access to for motivating reluctant readers into exploring the ideas, the other worlds, the information, the surprises, the sense of imagination contained inside the very books they too often disdain? What if these readers could find themselves engaged in a powerful book they couldn't put down? What would change in their reading lives? Would they forget their reading difficulties and simply read? Why are some teachers and parents able to find the right books for those children who are at a difficult stage in their reading lives? Why do some of us fail?

What Book Will We Read This Year?

Reading a book is a solitary act, a private affair in which we are walled off from present life, from the concerns that grab our attention and swamp our days. Yet school is a public place, and so the conflict begins: how do we engage twenty-five students in the silence of the reading moment; and what is it we are to teach them? Is just *reading* enough? The saying goes that it takes two to read a book, and often I as a reader am altered by my conversations with another reader of the same text, even if the responses of the other reader are in print form; I hear the voice of someone who has shared my text, and I rethink my experience. I see the film based on the book, and my thoughts about the story move in another direction. School can do this for youngsters, as long as we keep in mind that it is not the book we are teaching (because the teacher in the next school may be using an entirely different novel), but the understanding of how books work, how story lives, how artists create characters out of words, how our own lives are enriched by the new pathways that open between the pages. If this isn't why we force-feed students a diet of thick, old novels, why are we doing it?

It is eventually the reader's responsibility to be aware of the craft of the writer and the conventions that writers use, in order to have rich and fruitful experiences with literature. How many literary terms, works of art, epochs of literature should I teach my class? My answer as a teacher has to be as many as I can make matter to them, but that is where the negotiating, intervening, motivating teacher comes into play. Teachers are the mentors for youngsters in exploring how our literature works, but it is best if they guide and model, rather than teach and test.

41

Formulaic books, series books or books by an author who follows the same structure in each book are magnets for many readers, and build reading power and fluency. But how shall I classify the mystery novels that I save to read on airplanes? Are they a substratum of literature? I notice they get whole columns in the weekend book sections of some of our newspapers. My friends (male and female) who teach college like them, as does my friend who works with computers. I shall continue to read in this genre, while becoming more and more selective about my choices. And I read a wide-ranging variety of other texts, and that is one answer to meeting the needs of our students: not challenging them on the value of their personal choices, but offering them options, so that their selection becomes more varied, even more challenging. We show them possibilities, without demeaning their present literacy lives.

Consider the most popular novels, like Danielle Steele's or the Harlequin series. The romance books that many women read, and that we often mock, have values we often miss; those women readers are making their own choices, freed from family and job obligations, gaining power over their lives, even finding a sense of transformation in their lives, entering worlds far from their own realities, in the company of other women who, like themselves, find pleasure in stories of romantic fulfillment. Rather than criticize them for what they read, we would better serve them by driving them to the bookstore.

There are so many reasons for, purposes in, and ways of reading. A friend doesn't find the same satisfaction I did in a book I loaned her; I reread a childhood book and wonder why I ever enjoyed it, forgetting who I was and who I have become; a newspaper article saddens me, until someone else refutes the research; an article in a magazine causes my eyes to fill with tears as it forces my life associations to tumble out. I want the children we teach to know the possibilities that rich literacy processes can tap into, to know they can alter their futures, see the world from different viewpoints, construct their own views of ideals, transform their world pictures, own their lives, resist manipulation by corporations or governments, find pleasure and laughter and satisfaction in all types of texts, feel worthy as readers who make important choices, risk and fight for valued beliefs that will benefit all, be awake to the imagined possibilities that surround them. We aren't what we read; we read what we are, and what we can become.

Recently, a teacher asked me if there weren't a hierarchy of texts—beginning with the Bible or Shakespeare—and I asked her in return if a Mother's Day card from her son was worth anything; she agreed that we need to see a particular text in context before we assign it a seat in the room. When, as an agent of literacy support—parent, teacher, volunteer, friend—you remove judgment and refrain from being an arbiter of good taste, it becomes so much easier to help a reader make sense of a particular text, of the words, the structure, the ideas, the philosophy. That is why grandmothers and grandfathers are such enabling people in our lives; they are just there offering cookies and milk along with a book, minus the constant critique of our inadequate choices.

A Novel Defence

Recently, I was a guest on a radio program, along with a principal and his seventh-grade teacher, who had an all-boys class. The issue focused on the reading of novels, and the commentator announced that she and I were "the dinosaurs" in this discussion, locked into a long-ago past when children read what they were told to read, and novels were mandatory texts. The conversation on-air proceeded in an orderly way until the teacher announced that the he used no novels in his all-boys classroom because they didn't like reading them. Instead, he opted for magazines and newspapers, and he felt the boys were responding well to the new literacy resources. I was suddenly overwhelmed with sadness; these youngsters were being taught by a sensitive and compassionate young man who was robbing them of rich and varied literacy exploration, in the name of offering them what they really wanted. But most of what they wanted, they already had! The materials were either brought from home, or easily accessible in the school library. I celebrate the young teacher's attempts to build a relevant literacy program, but the job is more important than just offering students what they already know.

I certainly celebrate his inclusion of popular texts in his attempts at getting boys to read and reflect, but I have seen so many other teachers enrich their programs with texts that were new to the youngsters, or different from their standard reading materials, while at the same time building opportunities and respect for the resources that were "owned" by the students. I think it's a matter of negotiating the literacy territory, recognizing that every child has a right to read what he or she wants to read at some time during the day, but, as wise parents and teachers also know, we require the strength to ensure that the children experience texts that change their lives in different ways, scenes that make them laugh and cry, novels that portray lives so like or unlike their own, articles about science and geography and health that move them further into ideas and issues. We need ways of helping them meet these texts actively, as full participants in the literacy event, rather than as merely recipients of the teacher's wisdom. We know how to open these other complex genres to the interests of youngsters; we know that the culture of the classroom will determine the attitudes and behaviours of our students, and if we create a place for all types of texts, experienced and shared in engaging and significant ways, we can enlarge the literacy sphere of every child we meet. As teachers and librarians, we have magical powers that parents lack; they are weighed down with hopes and expectations and dreams and responsibilities and the demands of daily life, quite different from our professional approach to child care in the widest sense. My son's teachers often did what I couldn't, and sometimes I resented their successes when balanced against my failures. But together we raise the children, and classroom and school culture may determine how youngsters will approach each literary work.

I have had a dozen requests from high schools this year, concerning independent reading time—twenty minutes in the school day when everyone reads. Often I am told that even the secretary and the caretaker read, as if these employees would be exempted because of their status or lack of formal education, when they may spend more time reading texts than many of the teachers. I find this type of activity useful for motivating team spirit, for cheerleading the students into greater effort, but I wish there were occasions during that time for talking to others about what we have read, for asking others about their texts and their responses, for chatting with the teacher about his or her choice of material, for getting on the internet and searching for background details, or for more information on the time or place or culture or ideas that the writer had built her text around. Build me a culture of literacy, and I will rejoice in the independent reading initiative, but I do know that one-third of students are receiving no help in building literacy strategies, another third are just going through the motions, and only the last third are truly relishing the freedom from a restrictive literacy curriculum.

When my son was five years old, we took a holiday in Spain. The motel we stayed in had a pool, and I anticipated Jay's learning to swim alongside his dad. But he didn't, preferring to splash and play and run into the ocean's waves. When we returned, I enrolled him in my university's swimming program for kids, and we went to the first lesson. The instructor asked all of the parents to move up to the gallery away from the children's eyes and ears, which we did. The twenty children stood shivering by the edge of the pool, and the coach appeared—a young woman with very long hair. She jumped into the water, got her hair wet, swung it around her head, and shouted, "Who wants a ride to the deep end of the pool?" My son's hand shot up, and in five seconds, he was in the water, carried on the back of an Amazon. This image has stayed with me for twenty years, through Jay's membership in the high school swimming team, colouring my own understanding of how we teach/instruct/coach our children. We get into the pool and support their young bodies in the deepest waters. Then, and only then, can we really help them learn. I want coaches who lace up their own skates, catch the baseball, pitch a curve or ski downhill, and I want teachers who read real texts, write real thoughts, and share real feelings with youngsters, while at the same time valuing the learning. I still sit on the rug with the kindergarten class, although now they may have to help me up after the story!

While waiting for my car to be tuned at the auto dealership, I noticed the young man sitting beside me reading a poetry anthology, poems by Joseph Brodsky. I couldn't help but ask him about his choice of reading material, and he told me he was a professional bass player who had just moved to my city and found that poetry was a great calming influence during this transition in his life.

If we opt out of printed texts, what will we have omitted, even removed from the lives of our children? Do we show a film in class because it is easier than reading the book it was adapted from? How do we balance the immediacy of visual images with the power of printed texts? Do we opt out or add alternative literary modes to our kids' developing lives? We will not overcome illiteracy by ignoring the media in their lives and pushing books and magazines, nor will we build literate citizens by excluding reflective and aesthetic and informative printed texts. It is more difficult to read a book than to watch a film, but much depends on the nature of the experience and the context and the text itself. Did I choose it myself, or with my classmates? Is there a test for it? Do I have time to accomplish "reading" it? Does it require me to interpret and reflect and rethink my assumptions? Am I changed by what I see or hear or read?

For me, if the inquiry is significant, if the exploration of the topic is authentic, if the student is connected to the issues or themes or ideas being considered, then the learning will be woven together seamlessly. Reading as a process is unnoticed by the reader if the need to discover is strong; we read for a reason, whether it is a book, a newspaper, a film or a computer screen.

What role do books and authors play in our lives, and in the lives of our children at school and at home? How afraid is society of the power of books—we censor them, burn them, remove them, and often distrust their influence. Many religious groups are wary of certain books, and government officials in North America are usually drawn from business or law, seldom from the arts or education. We encounter anti-intellectualism in epithets like nerd or geek; elected officials, even presidents, sometimes flaunt their distaste for books and magazines. What models do youngsters see in their worlds encouraging or believing in the culture of books?

I'm Not a Kid Anymore!

And what of the art of the novel written especially for these students? "Young Adult" books by the thousands fill our libraries, our bookstores, our independent reading times, but never our classroom programs. Why the rush toward books for forty-year-old readers when you are fourteen? Why the pride in a parent or teacher's voice when they say, "My kids are only into adult books—no teenage stuff for them." I did introduce YA books to our teacher education program years ago, only to be reproached by a colleague who said, "We have a greater responsibility than literacy, and that is to bring the best of world literature to the students." In hindsight, I think I should have said, "Which students, the third who quit high school, the third who are bored and not doing well, or the third who would read that literature without us interfering?" But wisely, I crept back to my office and read the latest YA novels by Katherine Paterson and Jean Little, perfect models of humanity and talent.

I have read such gifted, wonderful writers in this YA world, creating well-told stories full of all the elements we seem to want our kids to experience, and I am hopeful that the millions of youngsters who are not reached by what we now teach can find something of worth in those artists who address them directly. I am so thankful for those librarians, both school and public, who find the books, read the books, stock the books, and celebrate the books with the young people they serve. They are our connection to the literature of the new world, and they will extend the literacy limits of so many, helping them move into the uncharted territories of powerful fiction. Teachers would do well to join forces with these knowledgeable, often unsung, literary masters. Perhaps the literacy future of young people will not be the same as our own pasts.

Many English teachers joined the profession because they were addicted to reading, because they believed in the power of literature and knew its potentially life-altering effects. They imagined sharing their love of books, and find it upsetting to teach students who are part of a generation that lives in a multi-modal literacy world, with little time for the literary treasures of the past. But we know teachers who have transcended the popular culture, who have transformed students from single-text readers to multi-text literate learners. School can be a place that alters the negative and disabling literacy behaviours and attitudes of its students, and literature can then become a valued mode of literacy, if youngsters are engaged with texts that connect first to their lives, and then to unknown worlds. Teachers who can re-imagine literacy and literature for the students they teach will enrich their lives forever. Students need to feel satisfied and rewarded by the experience of learning from within the literacy event. When that happens, they will come to see themselves as successful readers, learning more about the strategies proficient readers use as they work with more complex texts. They will build reading muscles because they want to change, because they have already seen results. They have begun to see themselves as book users, even book lovers.

It is so difficult to remember that people are reading in every country of the world, and that the books they read are not always the ones we read. Often we find translations of books from other cultures in English, and we wonder about the literature and the literacy lives of young readers in France, Brazil, Kenya, Sri Lanka. We are brought up short by the realization that so many of our students in large metropolitan areas bring those worlds with them, and we suddenly transport them into the literary history of North America, of Great Britain, of the English language, regardless of the cultural and social patterns that help them understand their lives. I would love to see an English unit of study made up of books translated from other languages, or written in English by authors who live elsewhere, especially in the genre of books for young adults. Virtual travel.

In my youth, most students didn't want to read the literature of school, but societal expectations were such that they complied. The dogma of school, the duty of spending time with books. We read them in the same way as we were forced to participate in Army Cadets. We did what we were told or we quit. What sends sales of a book through the roof today is not our teaching of it but the fact that it has been featured on Oprah, or a movie has been made from it. We need to continue the dialogue that many writers on education are engaging in, about our practice of literacy and our choice of literature, so that we can include the spontaneous pleasure of reading along with our strongly held beliefs in critical commentary and the craft of the writer. Many good teachers are doing this; they, as the gospel singer Mahalia Jackson reminded us, "live the life I sing about in my song." To teach the canon, you must believe in the canon; and not only that, you must continue to add to it, find new texts, celebrate them with the students, and joyfully read. The enthusiasm of the teacher is catching, and at least the kids will know what you stand for, what you value, and this will help them to develop their own text needs, not just now in class, but throughout life, as they study, work, marry or parent.

How Many Books Has Your Boyfriend Read?

When a young woman brings home a suitor to meet her parents, and her mother asks, "Is he a reader?" we know what she means—good, big novels, preferably written in the last century or two. That definition of reading is burned into our collective consciousness, because it represents so much of our value system concerning who we want our children to become, and education for many is focused on this one aspect of literacy, the sophisticated and urbane novel reader. Are we to blame television and other even newer media for this loss in the way we spend our leisure time, or have we added to the mix, rather than ignoring it? I remember sitting around the radio sixty years ago with my family in the evening, listening to programs that are even now replayed on smaller radio stations on Sunday evenings at 7:00 p.m.—*The Shadow, Fibber McGee and Molly,* and so many others. Now it may be a video film, watched by each family member alone in their room. Society changes, and so do the media with which we spend our time. Can we make room for books? Do we need to?

In this golden fantasy of a past, literature-enriched life, we paint our significant others holding books, but these texts have never just been fiction even in our imaginary utopias; they have always included books of information, biography, travel, cooking, religion, pictures, magazines and scrapbooks, and poetry anthologies and collections of letters from loved ones in our home country. But could these print texts not be seen onscreen, on small, battery-powered, book-like devices that we hold as we lie in our beds, lulling us to sleep, just as paperbacks used to do? For many of us, the feel of a book is too powerful a sensation to forego for a plastic replica, but that is what the young of today will know as reading material. Might we then be concerned with what is in the text, what it says, rather than with only the shape of the object, and with what the reader may do with what he has perceived? This way of thinking about literacy asks us to consider the relationship of the reader and the writer (or the viewer and the maker, or the listener and the musician); we wonder how the text is affecting the reader, what changes are happening, what new connections are being made, what biases are being revealed, what judgments are being formed, what understanding about this medium is being developed, what impact this literacy event is having upon the participant, what meaning is being made.

What if we find out from the young woman's new suitor the kinds of texts he reads or views or listens to, and the effect those vicarious experiences have on his life and on his relationships? As Joan Rivers says: "Can we talk?" A much better way to judge a man than by the books on his bookshelf that he may never have read. But this requires us to rethink what we mean by, "Is he a reader?" My simplistic solution is to always complete the statement: "Is he a reader...of what?" No longer does the word *reader* stand on its own; I need to know how he places himself in the world he is constructing. What resources is he surrounding himself with? How is he becoming aware of world events, of the reasons for our behaviours? How does he find out? Who helps with the choices that confront him? What makes him laugh and cry? What stories cause him to reach out?

Which songs will he memorize so that he can lift his voice with the choir?

What are you reading and watching and listening to? What does it mean to you? And how are you being changed? Or comforted? Or frightened? Or made stronger?

I was on an airplane recently, and a young, apparently newly-wed couple was boarding in front of me. The husband offered to place the bag his wife was carrying in the overhead compartment. He inquired as to what it was, and she replied, "Books." And he said "Books! Our new bookshelf is full!" And I understand his response. "Do we need more books? Why? We have the new TV with surround sound!" And he may be right. But what about all the people who fill their walls with books they read twenty years before? Have those become art or wallpaper? Do they create a sense of pride or satisfaction, or are they touchstones for a remembered past? Or are such people misrepresenting their present lives, as happens with the rich, leather-bound, never-read volumes that designers place in a living room for purely aesthetic effect? There is no doubt that books matter to many people; but to others, they are mementos of discomfort, even pain. What role does school play in determining the roles that books will hold in young people's lives? Any?

As a young male graduate left the halls of my faculty in June last year, he shouted out, "I never have to read a book again!" But recognize that after five years of university, he was tired of projects and research papers and essay-writing and independent reading and articles from arcane periodicals and journals and handouts and guidelines, and throw him some slack. Instead, let's wonder what he meant by *book* and by *read*, and take solace in the knowledge that he will need and want texts throughout his life, from Dr. Spock's manual on raising children, to the TV news reports on a recent war, to the medical journal about diabetes, to the picture books he reads aloud to his children over and over again, to the computer magazine he gets in the mail every month, to the blog he shares with his former classmates. What school can do is to give him the gift of literacy, to grace him with the freedom to be able to choose the texts that matter, with an understanding that he will make the meaning *with* these texts, interacting with the ideas and the information until he can make enough sense to move on. Will he discover fiction again? Of course. Will it be in novel form? Who knows? A story is a story when it is artfully told. Books will be there if and when he needs them (if they are friendly objects, and no one has made him afraid of them).

Do You Read Me?

When I use the term "literacy event," I don't mean only a curriculum lesson or a subject component, although meaningful examples of these events can often include formal, structured lessons. But most frequently, deep, meaningful meaning-making involving reading and writing texts grows from the engagement with the ideas that are being read and written about. When students are inside the experience, needing to read and write in order to come to grips with the issues and concerns being discussed or examined, when texts are being interpreted or constructed as part of the learning process, then I can sense that a literacy event is happening. The young person needs not only to inhabit the words and images, but to see herself as a performer of what she has learned, representing and owning the learning. In effect, she herself becomes the literacy. And she reads and writes with her whole self, with her body, with her emotions, with her background as a daughter and student and citizen; she sits in school beside her family members, and she reads every text she meets alongside them, inside her cultural surround. Literacy is constructed through identity.

We who see reading as a series of natural, everyday processes don't regard it as a singular event, a time-tabled, compulsory act that holds us back from things we want to do. To us, it's an invisible process that allows us entry to a thousand thoughts, whenever we want to or need to read whichever text we confront. We have learned the magic word: choice. We can choose what and when to read, how to skip the sections that hold no interest for us, when to stop reading an unsatisfying book and move to another text, to read something others may scoff at, which magazine to read depending on our mood, read anything and everything while waiting in the doctor's office, drift through a bookstore and browse the shelves, reread a book that our psyche cries out for, read while watching our children play hockey, become lost in a fictional world and lose track of time, spend hours searching on the internet for health information. Reading just happens as part of how we live our lives. Can we let reluctant, dormant readers in on this secret? Learning to choose, to select, may be the truth we have been seeking in our literacy teaching. The libraries are vast; the bookstore has two or three floors full of shelves; the magazine racks hold hundreds of periodicals, the internet goes on forever. Who will help young people become educated consumers, readers who know what they need, what they want, aware of personal choices that can free them from past fears of failure and disappointment?

Let's rewrite the curriculum to include the methodology of text choice, a way of thinking about literacy that might enable more youngsters to meet more texts than they had ever dreamed of.

3. Understand the use of technology as literacy.

Literacy and the Plugged-in Generation

I came to the world of the computer kicking and screaming. I saw no need for it, and I knew I had no aptitude. I was an absolute failure on the typewriter, and I paid typists to get my manuscripts ready for the publisher. I didn't take typing in high school; only girls in commercial courses were that fortunate. Everyone knew that we males would have secretaries—and then the earth shifted, secretaries disappeared, and I was left holding the keyboard. In the 1970s, when I was completing my graduate thesis, my friend Linda typed the manuscript fourteen times; she mentions it every time I see her. Today, with our friends *delete, cut,* and *paste,* we could have done it together without a worry in the world. Timing is everything.

When I had to teach my first course online, I once again had to hire a competent computer expert to sit beside me once a week and plug in my thoughts. None of the students knew, but I now wonder if they had friends sitting beside them. As computers became more user-friendly and I accepted them as a communicating tool, my life changed forever. I answer dozens of emails each day, search the internet whenever I need to, chat with my son at school in the States, and I wrote this very book with no one but me working the gas pedal and the brake.

Everyone I know working in the areas of education and literacy spends hours each day reading and writing on the computer, while celebrating the book as the most important centre of the child's world. But I am not so sure. For me, story still holds that honoured position, but the story may be electronic, about real life, and can even be sung with accompaniment on a synthesizer. The plugged-in world is here, and I am now an immigrant, while kids are native-born citizens.

Some schools have one computer at the back of each classroom, while others have a computer lab down the hallway; some have a trained librarian with print and computer resources to assist each teacher, and others have a portable computer for each student and a "smart board" for the teacher. I am so impressed with the ways in which schools have organized to give their students opportunities to become computer-literate—to learn about technology, but more important, to use technology to support and enhance their own learning events. But I remember my son's kindergarten class: there was one computer in the corner, and Jay's excellent teacher gave each five-year-old a chance to work with it once a week—and that was twenty years ago. However, there are terrible inequities in our children's computer education.

My son was my mentor in helping me become computer-literate, and I must confess that I am still a beginner. He, like others in his generation, views computers as a normal part of life's processes—nothing special. I have asked for his help hundreds of times, only to be told, "Dad, I've shown you that before." It put me in the place of the learner, and how it frustrated me! Now we have youngsters at all levels working with word processors, chat lines, blogs, emails, text messages, web searches, photoshop, etc. And all of these activities are literacy events. Boys and girls are reading and especially writing more than ever in the world's history. But what we can consider is the quality of the literacy events they are engaging in, the kinds of learning processes they are exploring, and what languaging options they may be minimizing, or even missing.

As I noted earlier, Bill Gates has stated that the only thing necessary for successful interactions with computers was literacy, and this makes teachers more significant than ever. What does that mean? We are the ones mandated to ensure that our children can make sense of the different codes they will encounter in life, the many modes and forms that will contain meaning, along with the understanding that the kids are the meaning-makers, and they will require the strategies and behaviours necessary for literacy success. A tall order, and schools are working hard to move toward that goal. But as teachers we encounter many obstacles, and we have to be tough and brave.

A recent newspaper column in the Toronto Star reported on sociolinguist Sali Tagliamonte's two-year study of more than one million words of text messaging between 71 Toronto teens. She found their unique shorthand not only forms just 2.4 percent of their online dialogue, it also shows a versatility and adaptability that may actually strengthen their command of the language.

The controversy deepens as new ways of encoding thought enters our literacy stronghold. What interests me is the fact that text messaging is here, and I am unable to read or write in this mode. But what a futile effort it would be to try and stamp it out. In a recent talk to teachers, I asked the audience to raise their hands if they use the new code in their own text messaging; many indicated that they did. Where is Shakespeare when you need him (except for all those arcane English words we no longer use, even in the most formal of writing. Ah, English changeth, methinks)?

I Liked the Movie Better

I have been a teacher, an educator of teachers, and a parent for many years, and I have witnessed enormous changes in the texts children use to make meaning, to construct their worlds. Children today have greater latitude for embedding their identity in a variety of texts. With computer programs, written text and visual texts can sparkle, move around the screen, produce music and movement; the player can freeze and navigate images, and move up a level at a time. In this way, readers not only adapt the visual information but also transform it. With computers, young people are constructing their own meanings and adapting to new forms.

Print texts such as picture books, basal readers, illustrated books, and pop-up books are artifacts which carry with them assumptions about readers, their gender, the way they will read books, and even the type of message they are expected to receive. They are not simply a means to an end; they are important tools in children's burgeoning development of literacy skills. As well, there are prescribed practices that accompany different texts, such as the way we read a biology book or a stock market report, rules embedded within each mode, and it is precisely our children's tacit understanding of them that we need to isolate and understand, in our developing literacy curriculum in different subjects and genres. Today we should be concerned less with understanding one type of written text than we are with mastering multiple modes and the practices implied in each one. Hence, we must concentrate less on the purely linguistic and more on the multi-modal.

What is of great importance here is that children are dealing with a greater network of meanings and our literacy curriculum needs to match that to set them up for the future. It is less about analyzing early readers specifically than it is about analyzing early readers' *future* with literacy. Or rather, the disparity between their future literacies (what they will have to read and produce) and what they are actually learning today in home and at school. Indeed, there is a pronounced difference between literacies children are developing at home and the literacy of schools. It is a divide that needs to be understood and explored. We need to rethink the way we learn to be literate, and the way we regard literacy and literate behaviour.

The disparities between the plugged-in, electronic bedroom and the traditional school contribute to the alienation many children feel about what goes on in their classroom. How can we build on their digital literacies as we reconceptualize how we could teach reading and writing in ways that would help them to value the intertextuality of the many different literacy experiences in their lives?

My friend Bonnie, who teaches fourth grade in Texas, runs the most amazing *e-pal* program, building on the *pen-pal* experiences of the past. For several years, her students have been writing back and forth to members of the armed forces serving on the ship *USS Essex*, based in Japan. The e-letters the sailors write, and the questions the children ask, let us view an authentic literacy process right in front of our eyes. The work is downloaded and made into booklets, and I am sure that each member of the two teams is proud of the results.

Many teachers reading these words may be shouting, "But we already have engaging, exciting programs involving computers in all aspects of our literacy programs," and I salute them. They are moving us all toward the future, and I hope that their stories will encourage the rest of us who work with children to accept the new role of technology in their young lives, and support them in all aspects of literacy growth. We can be plugged in at times, and still gather together and sit in a circle, to listen to a tale 2,000 years old.

On a recent visit to a grade four classroom, I read aloud to the students several poems about nature from my anthology *Images of Nature*, and, as usual, I was impressed with their young minds' abilities to connect their lives and imaginations to the images created by the poets and the artists whose work illustrated the text. I find on these occasions that the less I say, the more the children give me. What I must do, though, is remain completely in the present, and listen carefully to the spontaneous ideas that the work generates, and then help frame their thoughts so that we can find more meanings together.

At the end of the session, feeling pleased with myself, I was asked by a boy if I had heard of the woman who lived in a tree. When I said I had not, he told us a bit about her, and then suggested that he would get some information together and courier it to me. He was eight years old.

Three days later, a package did indeed arrive at my desk, containing a complete dossier of printouts of articles and photographs about this woman, along with a table of contents, a summary the boy had written from the printouts, his reflections on the event, and a collage he had made from the colour photos he had downloaded from different websites. Welcome to the world of digital information.

In 1992, there were fifty websites. As I write this, in 2006, there are ninety-three million.

Watching a TV news program recently, I saw a video of a school in China using "paperless books," the boys and girls each with a hand-held screen print device. What does all this mean for young people in the future, and are we preparing them well enough?

The Mouse in Everyone's House

As parents and educators, we know we can no longer view the texts we use during literacy teaching as necessarily primarily written or linguistic—they are also made up of images, of sounds, of movement. The texts that students read and enjoy at home are print and electronic. Our choice of texts in the classroom needs to reflect the multi-modality seen on the web and in CD-Roms to appeal to students' reading behaviours. Yet computer use can be balanced by programs involving print resources that connect the students to the worlds they inhabit, while at the same time stretching their abilities and interests: we can include novels, biographies, poems, columns, and articles that represent the best writers we can find who will enrich the lives of our students. Resources that touch the emotions and the intellect have a much greater opportunity for moving readers into deeper frames of understanding. Aesthetic knowledge lets us see further and sense the "as if," the hallmark of thoughtful, mindful citizens, as the education philosopher Maxine Greene puts it.

New technologies both allow us and encourage us to connect with learning partners all over the world. There is a mouse in almost everyone's house that permits us to make contact with others who share or debate our ideas, our philosophy, our questions, and our investigations. To enter into the essential concerns of the issues in life that matter, the questions that the arts, history, and sciences raise and ponder, we must become sufficiently proficient in the literacies that different disciplines require. And we become better and better at working within a specific literacy as we practise using it and refining the way we use it. For example, we begin to understand how a scientist thinks and behaves as we act like one—wondering, observing, asking questions, taking careful notes, writing up our conclusions. But the secret of our success as literate people really lies in our common reason for needing the tools of literacy. I want to understand how to be a learner, how to approach the world and find things out, discover how things work, figure out why people behave as they do, learn to interpret, report, respond critically, and creatively, summarize, find ways of representing ideas and opinions and feelings through the arts. As I use a particular literacy's code and schema, I become more familiar with how it functions. I can begin to see how the bits and pieces fit together in order to make the most meaning.

Technology does not necessarily improve the acquisition of literacy in and of itself. It requires carefully crafted learning programs focused on creating dynamic opportunities for the interpretation, manipulation, and creation of ideas in the classroom. The rapid development of the internet is a little like a gold rush: some miners find gold, but many find failure.

In terms of literacy teaching, our students are not learning to be literate the way we did or the generation before us did. As my colleague Ruth McQuirter Scott has said, "As an educator, a writer, and a parent, I struggle to keep up with the dizzying pace of technology. There's a revolution taking place under my nose and trying to understand it is like taking aim at a moving target. I don't dare stand still, since this generation of children will simply move on without me. I'd hate to miss the show!"

Mining for Gold

Recently, I was working with a grade seven/eight teacher and her class on a social studies unit on mining. It was such a pleasure to explore this relevant and significant issue alongside such an experienced educator, who had embraced technology as a literacy medium. The resources that she had gathered for the exploration with the students represented multi-literacies at their best. She had worked with the school librarian beforehand to locate and display as many print and visual resources as possible, and the collection was full of informative types of texts, from oral histories to folksongs about mining, from poems to contemporary non-fiction accounts of mining disasters.

But what caught my attention was the computer teacher, who had also been part of the planning sessions. In this school, each student and teacher had a laptop computer, and each teacher had a smart board, an interactive large screen whiteboard that helps integrate digital information into teaching, presenting and brainstorming. Teachers and students are connected through their computers, and can write and share notes, insert diagrams, link to websites and save the work for future use. I was in the middle of the future, and everyone was plugged in.

The study involved their working sometimes in small groups, sometimes with partners, as well as independently, researching and exploring different aspects that the class had brainstormed concerning mining, both in North America and internationally.

Their inquiries took them places I had not thought of, not just geographically, but philosophically and culturally. Some of their research involved paper texts- documents, stories, songs- but most were connected to the Internet.

Different students worked on different areas of interest:

- types of mining carried on today;
- a map of the mining locales using the computer satellite mapping program;
- accounts of disasters from newspaper sites, statements of
- safety regulations from government and mining officials, union mandates;
- email and chat-line interviews with both retired miners and mining officials;
- politicians' promises to ensure safety for the miners;
- interactive notes to each other with added information or queries;
- maps, diagrams, and pictures scanned into computers;
- continual comments from the social studies teacher and the computer teacher, with suggestions, resources, assessments, personal observations, and reflections;
- e-portfolios of their work, categorized and organized.

There were other IT experiences, but as a drama teacher I found their presentations very powerful. They made use of Power Point, of course, but as well they had written and shared monologues portraying different people involved in mining operations over the years, along with poems they had found and poems they had written, accompanied by two boys with guitars, with visuals shown on a screen.

As a guest in the classroom, I summed up the event with a reading of long excerpts from Cynthia Rylant's new book, *Ludie's Life*, in which she chronicles the life of a miner's wife through almost a century of living in a mining town. It is a profoundly moving story, and the work the students had engaged in during the previous month enriched their listening, and provided them with background and information to bring to Rylant's words meanings and emotional responses deeper than any series of individual lessons could achieve. This group of students were inside the new literacies, and they had taken me and the two teachers with them on the journey into the darkness of a deep, deep mine. They had shone their lights and shown the way.

4. Remember that story is the heart of literacy.

The Tale, the Teller, the Telling, and the Told

But what of stories, the ones we remember reading in our rooms, perhaps in our schoolrooms, those narratives we still remember with affection? Will technology only be about information? At an annual conference for teachers working at the International Schools in southern Asia, this year held in Sri Lanka, I had finished my talk and was collecting my books when the teachers began lining up to purchase them, since new resources in English were hard to come by in their countries. I ended up giving all the books away, hoping they would enrich the lives of students in the different countries represented at the conference. When my supply had been cleaned out, the young man who was putting away the chairs asked if there was one left for his family; he had no books in his house. I had a new one still in my book bag, and it became his. We take it for granted in our teaching communities that there will be resources—perhaps not plentiful, and not all that we would want, but enough to work with—to fill the lives of our children. I remember a school in a remote village in India where an ingenious teacher of ten- to twelve-year-old boys had only one book: he ripped the pages from it and gave one to each boy, who then "owned" his page for two or three days, after which the class heard the whole tale told by the readers, page by page.

The true gift of the picture book is its appeal to both adult and child. Side by side, we share the words and the images, each of us building our own story, the child lost in the telling, the adult warmed by the book-engendered relationship. We can find thousands of picture books to choose from, and we should feel free to read the ones that we appreciate, that we want to share, since the students are keen observers of our feelings.

I read Jane Yolen's *Owl Moon* to a class of student teachers as a means of setting the mood for a lesson on poetic language, but their responses to the book took us in a different direction. Her gentle memoir about the effect of the silence of the woods on a parent and child on a winter's night resulted in my students reminiscing about their childhoods; they told stories of camping with their own families, swimming at a cottage with cousins, canoeing with their dads, bird-watching in the marsh. I asked the students to write down their memory stories and email them to me, and I put them together in a book which I had copied and distributed at the last class of the final term. The students remained long after class, reading the stories of the classmates with whom they had spent a year as beginning teachers, transported into a picture-book forest they had each suddenly recognized as their own.

In our contemporary world, opportunities for experiencing storytelling are often missing in the lives of many children. Aside from television's passive, non-interactive storying, some children hear no stories read aloud or told until they go to school. With broken families, crowded schedules, new curricula, and urban development comes the tragedy of children without a storehouse of stories. Grandparents who might have told stories may be unavailable or live far away; the home may not be a storying place; television and computers may dominate and limit talk time; parents may be shift workers; single parents may lack time and energy for sharing stories; storytelling may not be considered a significant experience by the adults in the home. It may be that school will have to bear the burden of story on its shoulders, that teachers will be the storytellers who reach most children.

We know that things happen to people when they hear stories, that any theory about the place of story in schools has to begin with this fact. Story is not an exercise in explanation or persuasion, but an experience between the teller and the told. How a storyteller feels about an event can determine how (or if) it is remembered. The emotional intensity of an experience will influence the way memory is affected by the storytelling. In considering a story truth, we need to attempt to understand what the teller might have been feeling, thinking, and doing at the time of the experience, as well as the context of the telling—who is listening and why, and what the consequences of the telling will be. And, I have to add, the tale we choose to tell can determine who listens and why, and the context for the telling can make or break both the teller and the effect of the telling on the told. In storytelling, everything matters: the tale, the teller, the telling, and the told.

Given the opportunity, children come to know the anatomy of story—its forms, genres, motifs, patterns, universals, words, and images. Story acquaints kids (even those who do not or cannot read) with a variety of language patterns, some of which may be outside their language community. It can familiarize them with literary language, an awareness they will need as readers and writers. And the words that are found in story—where else would a child meet them? Words from other times and places, words found only in print, shared by storytellers with magic literary storehouses, idioms, expressions, metaphors, allusions—all to be met and savoured, some to be retained in the mind's eye.

Children today need to learn tolerance, understanding, and getting on with others, and storyteller Bob Barton says that among the best examples of stories that emphasize these qualities are the world's folktales. These "stories of the tribe" provide strong reading and listening materials for children. The context of "long ago" enables children to explore a variety of problems and concerns that have troubled humanity forever, but in a safe, non-threatening framework. The deeds of heroes, the schemes of tricksters, the lore of nations past, can all serve as complements to children's own development, in family situations, societal difficulties, supernatural beliefs, and natural phenomena.

I tell my story. You retell it, with all of your own life experiences playing upon it, and suddenly it's your story. Then we tell our two stories to a third member of the story tribe, who listens to both and builds a new, personalized version that shocks us with its own twists and turns, and causes us to re-cognize our selves. And we are present at the birth of a new story; we now have three for our story bag, and every time I choose one of those stories to share, I will unknowingly, unwittingly include bits and scraps from all of them and suddenly I am telling a different story, but it is still mine, and the story is inside, outside, and all around my head. Such is membership in the story culture. We tell our own stories—our daydreams, our gossip, our family anecdotes. We become human through our stories.

Read Me a Story; My Mind Is Tired

Can we capture the spirit of bedtime reading in a modern classroom, with students from so many different home settings, attitudes shaped by years of feeling worthless when confronted with print forms that seemed unreadable? Will they let me read out loud to them? Is it a worthwhile teaching strategy? The answers are simple: we can, they will, and it is. Still, it will take courage on your part, and stamina as you build the ritual. But you don't have to do all the work yourself: consider books on tape, radio programs that share items read aloud, speeches that matter, newscasters reading the news each night on television, and, most interesting, teenagers downloading the lyrics of their music so they can read them as they sing along. It is normal in our world to hear texts read aloud. Each year, student teachers tell me their stories of teachers who had read to them in different grades—picture books, novels, biographies, poems. Sometimes a novel took too long and they lost interest; sometimes they begged the teacher to continue long into the afternoon. In my role as a guest in schools, I have read aloud to hundreds of thousands of students in different settings around the world, and each time is like the first one: even though I always worry that they may not enjoy what I choose to read, that they may not listen to me, or will have nothing to say in response, the story is always there to support me, and to grab the children by the throat. I am often asked why I sometimes choose tough tales, with so much conflict and violence, even in the humour. It's because I want the children to turn around and face me, and join in the ceremony of the tale, the teller, the telling, and the told. Once we are inside the story circle, I can risk other types of text, more subtle, more nuanced; that is why I never bring just one book to a group; I prefer a set of selections, texts that fit together as they appear, one after the other, until the children want to add their own words to the mix, contribute their own responses. Excerpts from novels, three poems in a row, a picture book with dark and intriguing illustrations. These are all in my book bag.

I no longer worry about a child who hasn't yet joined; if I persist, he will come round, if not this time, then next time. I ignore the teacher who climbs over the children in order to silence the boy who is tickling his neighbour. But I must confess I was quite put off when a group of teachers placed their chairs amid the children in the gym, facing them with their backs to me, so that they could maintain order. If the story and the storyteller can't pull them in, time to retreat to the classroom.

When limited readers listen to text read aloud, sometimes the fear of the print starts to melt, to dissipate with the realization that they are understanding what they are hearing. There is a general rule in literacy: if a child can understand the text as he hears it read aloud, then he does not have a comprehension problem; he has difficulty with printed text. I found a boy in one elementary school in fifth grade whose reading disability was so acute that he couldn't read or write his name. His teachers were working with him, and he was positive about school and his attempts at becoming a reader. The amazing part of this story is that he was able to discuss at length the three novels his teacher had read to the class throughout the year, and his comments about the books were deeply structured and heartfelt. He had "read" the books.

I think back to a day at a school in Toronto when I worked with a group of 250 or 300 adolescents. They were so boisterous before I began that I wondered how I would get their attention and, once gotten, how I would keep it. In about 30 seconds, the story had them calm and listening intently. But the secret is there isn't any secret and that is partly the trick. Students have to see you immediately as who you are, what your job is, and to recognize what you have to offer. You strip yourself to the essence of teacher: "I am here to be with you, so that together we can do more than you can do by yourself. That is all I am here for. What I have for you are stories that matter to me and we'll share them and see if they matter to you. I have no idea if they will or not." The wonderful thing about working with large groups is they need to have that single focus, and the focus has to be one that connects them. They're not staring at you; they are in a space with you. I think that is what all of my teaching should be. "We have a visitor today, class, and he has some interesting things to share with you, and he cares a lot about you and we're going to have a relationship with him for an hour and a half." That is what I struggle to do with them. There is no big barrier between the students and me. I haven't got anything to put between me and them. I just have me.

How to Read Aloud

- Read aloud as a salesperson: choose several new books from the library and share excerpts from each, so that the youngsters will want to read them on their own.
- Read aloud as a traveller: share stories and information from other cultures, other places, other times. Let readers meet words and expressions from England, Australia, Sri Lanka, and translations from other languages.
- Read aloud as an expert: choose texts that are unfamiliar to the readers, more difficult than they might be able to manage on their own, so that their ear-print continues to be challenged.
- Read aloud as a researcher: use the content of different subjects as resources for sharing excerpts, anecdotes, observations, and reflections from newspapers, articles, and additional resources that you and the students find.
- Read aloud as a bard: chant and sing the poems and ballads of the past and present, and ask the youngsters to join in the refrains.
- Read aloud as a storyteller: retell a story that you know well or want to learn. Freed from the printed text, you can move and gesture, and alter your voice to bring the text alive.
- Read aloud as an actor: choose a role in a script or a readers' theatre selection, and model passionate and energetic voices.
- Read aloud as an editor: select revised and completed writings from the youngsters, practise them, and share

them in a public reading, adding significance to their words with your careful reading.

- Read aloud as a lover of print texts: choose things from your own life to read to the kids—a column from the newspaper, bits from a course you're taking, a letter from a friend who lives far away, an excerpt from a book you loved as a child, the picture book you once read to your son or daughter.

Forty years ago I began teaching literature and drama in a school with twenty classes on a rotary system, where one group after another would appear in my classroom every forty minutes—eight classes a day. I found hope and strength in story, stumbling, as it were, into "storying for a living." To involve students (and to save my life) I began to explore all the ways and means of having the children work with stories. The students were retelling them, reading them aloud, writing from them, dramatizing them, arguing about them, finding other stories like them, other versions, other authors, and telling each other their own personal stories.

The stories came in all shapes and sizes (life stories, novels, tales, home stories, gossip, retellings, legends, picture books, poems, scripts, advertisements). I had not yet acquired much understanding of why storying was so important for children, but it worked in my classroom and so I continued.

Over the years, the understanding of storying has increased dramatically, and now we are able to be selective and adventuresome in handling narrative with young people. Since I moved into working with teachers in both in-service and pre-service courses, story has retained its place at the centre of my work. Now we have dozens of books by informed authorities on why story matters, why we should help children engage in "storying." As well, we can now find stories of all kinds inside and outside the curriculum.

Educator Wayne Booth says that who we are is best shown by the stories we can tell, and who we can become is best determined by the stories we can learn to tell. The classroom is a village of stories and storymakers. The teacher, as well as the students, belongs to it; we, too, have stories to tell.

Lattes and Literature

As a child, I relied on the mobile library for my books, as it arrived at my school every other week. In my memory, I see very few boys inside the van, but I never missed a visit. The father of one of my girl friends drove the mobile library van, and I remember her parents' apartment overflowing with books he brought home. Can you imagine my pleasure when I read in today's newspaper a report about two bookmobiles in Toronto that service 1,000 people who check out 2,500 items a week. They visit 32 sites each week in parts of Toronto without library access. The US now has cybermobiles, equipped with computer work stations as well as books. Hurray for the old made new, for dedicated literacy support staff in our communities.

And think how libraries have changed over the centuries. Maureen Sawa, in her new work *The Library Book*, chronicles the history of libraries, and enriches our print lives. She reminds us that "people have been writing about the world around them for more than five thousand years, pressing marks into wet clay, chiseling letters into stone, or entering keystrokes into a computer, providing us with information about where we've been as we move forward into the future."

- The library of Alexandria was the most famous one of ancient times, but not the first, and most of its famous scrolls were written in Greek, copied by scribes from those in Athens and other important cities.

- Chinese libraries began in 550 BCE, but were destroyed by the first emperor, Shi Huangdi, in order to have complete control over the intellectual resources of the people.
- In tenth-century Persia, one official used five hundred camels to carry the books he owned, and the camels walked in line so that the books were in alphabetical order.
- The most used library in the world, next to Hong Kong's, is the Toronto Reference Library, and it's the banks of computers that families are grateful for.
- Today, online, we have access to digital libraries throughout the world, from 50,000 manuscripts and artifacts from the Silk Road, the centuries-old trade route between China and Europe, to every newspaper printed internationally. My own university library is planning on digitalizing 50,000 volumes this year.

For many children, the only bookstore in their lives is the rack at the supermarket, but be careful not to devalue that experience. I unthinkingly purged my son's shelf in his room of those Disney-type books acquired through birthdays and book fairs, only to encounter his sadness at the loss of childhood artifacts that held part of his literacy heritage. He has helped me to accept the books that matter to him and to me; sometimes our dreams converge, but when they don't, I leave space on the shelves for all of our choices, arranged in random order, like our experiences with the books that hold on to us forever.

Today, in large urban centres, we have giant book emporiums, where a reader can sit in a comfy leather chair, sip at a double latte, and peruse three or four new books. Many of the male customers are in the magazine section, lined up like men at urinals. I miss small, intimate bookstores, but I can happily lose myself among the thousands of texts at these book marts. And we are so fortunate to have dedicated librarians like my friends Ken Sedderington and Ken Roberts to fulfill our hopes with a wide range of options, along with wonderful school librarians, who, the newspapers tell us, are making a return to many schools after several years of understaffing. Where do you spend time among books and magazines?

If you have no pool at home, you swim in your neighbour's, if you're fortunate enough to have such luck on a hot summer's evening. I need book neighbours to invite me to join them in the literary waters. My friend Larry shares the *New York Times* book section every Sunday, and I relish each new article and review. Often I don't need to read the book; the in-depth review fills me up. My friend Joan takes me to the mystery bookstore once in a while. In my city, Toronto, I visited the Children's Bookstore for twenty-five years, and Judy and Marion and the staff enriched my life with the best books for children. When I think of its loss, I weep, until I look at the new baby stores springing up, like Maria's Tinlids. I find John and Leonard's Theatrebooks the most beautiful bookstore I have come across, specializing in books about theatre, film, media, and teaching the arts. For years, my son and I took in a movie every Friday night, and then on the way home stopped at a nearby bookstore located in a basement, and each of us bought a book or a magazine, feeling as if we were locals living in the Village in Manhattan; he still smiles when he remembers it.

If you live in a small town, are books available? Do the children in the school belong to a book club, and does the staff make sure that everyone can afford a book? Amazon.com has shipped books to every hamlet and village in my country—an electronic bookstore, at the press of a key. I need all kinds of texts to end my day–on my night stand, my coffee table, my kitchen counter, my desk, in my briefcase or my car trunk.

Books abound.

Books around.

Books galore.

5. Help students build strong reading muscles.

Comprehending Comprehension

I have never understood workbooks (or worksheets) filled with comprehension exercises. Often, the selections we had to read offered little meaning and no artistic merit, and what was it they were supposed to achieve? Similarly, most novel study units incorporated dozens of questions to be answered by the poor reader, none of which seemed to interest or pique the reader's curiosity, or, much more important, arouse an emotional or connecting response, never mind jump-starting the imagination. Years ago, reading expert Charles Reasoner taught me to help readers to *reveal their comprehension,* and that turned me around. I knew what I could do to assist a child in growing as a reader, for together we could reveal our thoughts, our ideas, and our feelings about a selection we had read. Then, together, we would enrich and extend each other's perceptions and perspectives about the text, deepening our understanding of how the writer and we readers made meaning together. I have never looked back. Attempting to understand a text holistically seems to incorporate into the literacy process everything that matters in teaching *reading* in the truest sense. In fact, everything matters in making meaning with the ideas composed by a writer/artist, especially our own experiences.

We are part of the process of comprehending a text. We matter; everything matters. Perhaps we need to use the term *spiritual literacy*. I will read/comprehend at the deepest level that touches my soul.

Reading is a social, meaning-driven act, and the reader has a purpose in mind for engaging in the process. As readers, we interact with the text (and the author), both the reader and the text forming a relationship that is integral to the meaning-making in a particular context. Always the reader's experiences and the textual meanings held in the code, and in the way it has been constructed, work together to determine the interpretation that will result from the reading. All the while we are bringing ourselves to the page, using our own personal schema to determine what we think about what we have read. Our negotiations with a particular text float on a continuum, depending on the function of the task and the implications of the reading. Sometimes we want exact data from a text, but in literature, our lives contribute such vital information as to affect the meaning being made. We depend on the interdependent interaction of all of our resources to make textual meaning, including our feelings and our spirits. We read from our complex lives.

Are our goals in teaching meaningful comprehension attained by:

- teaching or testing?
- increasing or decreasing understanding?
- expanding or contracting meanings?
- connecting to or disconnecting from the text?

Readers do not work through literal levels, move to inferential predictions, and conclude with critical generalizations. Instead, they work in a non-linear fashion, changing their judgments as they glean information and discover implications, anticipating and adjusting their predictions as the context deepens. All these processes are components of higher-order thinking, the guesswork that leads to broadened consciousness. We must design classroom activities that will provide opportunities for using various thinking processes when young people engage with print.

A reader's fluency is dependent on practice—lots of reading. For students in school, time for reading must be a major focus of the program. Readers bring their unique personal concerns to interact with the text on all levels. The teacher's role is to empower students to wander inside and around the selection, to wonder about it, to make meaningful connections, to deepen their picture of it. With the teacher as lifeguard and coach, students can safely explore the text and relate the ideas they find in it to their own lives, the author to the text, what other students see to what they see in their own minds, the patterns in the text to those in others, its world to the world of the moment. Forging such links to learning helps kids become readers.

Some story worlds are easy for us to enter: we have seen that mountain; we have lived in that city; we have known those bulrushes; we have owned a dog like the one in the book. Others are more difficult: we need the deft author who invites us in, the clever storyteller who draws us along, or the perceptive teacher who builds a context for us. As we hear or read the words, we transform those symbols into startling pictures that let us see into the story.

Comprehension is so easy to assess. Did the child laugh or weep? Was she surprised? Scared? Did she check on the flyleaf to see who wrote this text? Did the reading remind her of one of her life stories that illuminates her connection to the text? Did she want to find another story by the same writer? Did she talk to you about what she had read? Did she discuss her own sense of personal readership?

I Found My Dad inside My Book

My son came home from grade nine excited about his history class: "Dad, did you know that Caesar isn't just a salad?" Now we laugh together at that school memory, but the incident highlights how we can only recognize what we have somehow met before. Our knowledge is built from and based on all we have met, and those connections are being made all the time, consciously and subconsciously.

For example, when we are wholly engaged with a book, we bring the sum total of our life to the meaning-making experience; our previous experiences, our background knowledge concerning the content of what we are reading, our connections to the other "texts of our lives"—other books, other computer programs or the songs that are suddenly conjured up, our emotional state as we read, our knowledge of the nature of this particular text—how it works, the author's style, and the events of the world at large that are somehow triggered or referenced by our reading. Our main goal as literacy teachers must be to help students build bridges between the ideas in the text they are reading and their own lives by helping them to access the prior knowledge that is relevant to making meaning with the text, the information that life experience has retained and remembered in the brain, sometimes accompanied by emotional responses or visual images. When we give students a framework for understanding how they can enhance their own reading by activating their own connections, we offer them a reading strategy for life.

In my work in the teaching of reading strategies, I am seldom satisfied unless the learning stretches outside the classroom lives of the children, connecting our reading to broader world issues, so that our perspectives and our assumptions are challenged or altered. I am grateful to Paulo Freire, the Brazilian educationalist who was perhaps the most influential thinker about education in the late twentieth century, with his emphasis on dialogue and his concern for the oppressed, for giving us the expression "reading the word, reading the world." Somehow, when we read powerful, significant texts, we travel outside ourselves, exploring what lies beyond our immediate neighborhood, extending our vision, and awakening our personal and cross-cultural meaning-making. A grade eight class was preparing to read *The Ghost Train* by Paul Yee, and I asked them who had built the railway across Canada. Several students agreed that it was Germans, and when I asked why, they talked about the industrial force of that country and linked it with the world of giant steam trains. When I told them that Chinese boys not much older than they had been used as labourers, they were completely surprised, and moved into the book with a very different mindset.

All kinds of connections whiz through our minds as we read a text, and these can lead to fascinating explorations, but generally we want to model and support those that promote deeper insights into what we will read or have been reading. However, those leftover reminiscences and queries may prove to be powerful resources for writing in our response journals or during a writing workshop, where they can be developed and extended into thoughtful writing events. Reading is still a powerful resource for writing; the printed thoughts jiggle and bump against our own, drawing on ideas from the head to the pen (or keyboard).

Images in My Head

I grew up listening to radio dramas and comedies in which the air waves delivered the images to my mind, aided by the sound effects, the narrator, and the actors. Of course, when we read, a similar process occurs, and we picture much of what the print suggests, making movies in our heads as we read. And these images are personal, each one of us building a visual world unlike any other. Reading words causes us to see pictures,

81

which is understandable, since words are only symbols, a code for capturing ideas and feelings. But our imaginations work no matter the surrounds, and we see the world the print suggests.

As teachers, we need to model our own literacy with our students as often as possible. We can share portions of our reading lives with our students. We all remember teachers who read us a letter they had received, who read an editorial from a newspaper about an issue they cared deeply about, who showed us the novels they were reading or the books they had found about a hobby.

The teachers in my graduate courses write about their literacy lives, and I'm often moved by their recollections of their parents' interactions with books, the struggles of immigrant families who couldn't read in either their native or their adopted language, of homes where books were either invisible or sacred, where book learning was the only way to open doors. I hope that teachers will share some of their own life tales about reading with their students, so that we can all shed some of the elitist trappings and myths surrounding literacy.

I work in English. We do have a heritage of English literature, a body of work that we want children to experience. I recently came back from Mexico where they're struggling to get their national authors known in schools. I'm not advocating the cultural literacy that some elitists advocate. I'm after the right to read what you want and need to read, and the right to be thoughtful about and critical of what you read. I'm also aware that the better the text you interact with, the more meaning you're going to make. I don't want to alienate young people or demean their choices in books and magazines, but I do want to open them up to other options. If they're reading sports pages, they can read sports books by the same writers, or books about sports writers, or reviews of some of the articles they encounter. We can choose skateboarding, for example. There are all kinds of magazines about skateboarding. I'm not advocating that children who like Pokemon only read Pokemon cards, but understanding why they want to read Pokemon or skateboarding magazines is important. We have to know how a child's literacy mind functions if we want to help that child move ahead in acquiring his literacy passport stamps.

Consider the importance of critical literacy on the internet. Students are surfing the web and constructing their own individualized texts, evaluating sites, processing information, and interpreting data, so that they can connect themselves to the world. I think critical literacy is now being seen as a mainstream strategy. But I notice that teachers often have students attack the text rather than negotiating with and being enriched by it. We may have to find a new term for "criticism." "Critical," in so many people's eyes, means the negative side. I want to incorporate critical theory in all its aspects.

I would rather call it teaching for social awareness. Where is this story from? It is about bullfighting. Where and why is it popular? A publisher I stayed with in Mexico told me his son had been killed in a bullfight. I'm not going to criticize bullfighting in front of that father; to do so would be inappropriate. The context of literacy is everything. We read texts from the frameworks of our own lives.

Philosopher Maxine Greene teaches us to allow texts to enter our lives, to respond from experience, then listen to others responding. We can then begin to realize, for example, that other readers have a more intimate knowledge of the material in a given text than we have. I want to enter their circle and see why. I think the social side of literacy should be a primary concern for schools. How are we ever going to participate fully in society if we don't share our views? To have a single view from a teacher, taken from a manual, leaves little opportunity for the individual to consider other possibilities.

Each perspective must be analyzed and reflected upon. I need to talk about why a reader feels a certain way, what is going on in her mind, and what the storyteller is feeling. That triangle of making meaning is the focus of literacy.

In a school where the teacher may teach 130 students on a rotary timetable, it may be difficult to remember that it isn't the novel he or she is teaching, but what the novel represents, what an author is attempting to do, what tools the author will use to accomplish the goal, the context in which the book was written, the cultural and gender implications, why the story resonates with some readers and not others, why the novel was selected by the teacher.

What stories do you remember from childhood, from adolescence?

Which ones will you present to your children, your students?

Which stories help you to understand other stories, for these may be the true treasures. While my parents belonged to the Book of the Month Club when I was a child, my mother's favourite book was Mrs. Wiggs of the Cabbage Patch, by Alice Caldwell Hegan, published in 1901, about a single mother who raised eight children by taking in washing to stop the foreclosure of her home. At a time just after the Depression, when there were no automatic washing machines, when scrubbing boards were necessary, when clothes were hung outside on a line, when Eleanor Roosevelt (a family hero) promoted the book, when life was hard, the story rang with more than sentimental meaning for her. I read it as a child, and today I did an internet search and found dozens of sites, including one for a 1934 film that had been made. Why the interest in this old book? My memory takes me back and back, to washday in my childhood home, to all those family novels centuries ago, to the Girl of the Limberlost who had no shoes for the dance. Cinderella, let me ride in your coach.

6. Value the reading responses of young readers.

The Great Gatsby Fails English

My eleventh-grade English teacher survived by increasing the fear quotient of his teaching: everyone spent the year terrified he might call on them. During an inquisition about the novel *The Great Gatsby*, he asked me to explain the symbolism of the flashing green light at the end of the dock. I hadn't even noticed a flashing green light when I had dutifully read the book, and I muttered some inane comment. What I wanted to talk about was the 1949 film version I had just seen on television; it seemed to me that Alan Ladd had truly become the lead character, and the book's words and the film's images had blended together in my own interpretation. In my imaginary conversation with my teacher, we chatted about the time of the story, when my parents would have been teenagers, far removed in their poverty-stricken lives from the tennis courts and white suits of the people inhabiting that make-believe world. I wanted to ask him about his place in the literary history, for he would have been at university in Jay Gatsby's day. Could he have met him there, on the tennis courts, in the classroom, with people in smart white suits? I might have noticed the symbolism as we talked. He might have pointed out other details to me, and helped me see why they mattered. But he remained distant, a victim of his formal, unanswerable questions, except that, of course, his superior intelligence knew all the answers, taken from those who had passed that way before.

During that year, the teacher was absent for a month. His replacement was a student teacher, Mrs. Brooks, tall, blonde, and ethereal. We wrote poems for the month, and stared at her, and loved school. And yet I still admire our regular teacher—his self-confidence, no doubt a façade, and his genuine love for his English texts, if not for us or our concerns. Sadly, I can't remember any English teacher asking me about my own thoughts or feelings concerning a text we were studying, and as students we never talked about the texts outside school. They seemed so irrelevant.

And yet, I have just finished an article reviewing two new books about the life and times of Benjamin Disraeli, a past prime minister of England, and rushing from my memory was a play that we studied with that teacher, so far from our small town in Ontario, about political scheming a century before. My connection had been made, and I read the article twice. I would have phoned the teacher, but he is no longer with us.

"Can I read a magazine in class, Sir?"

"Of course you can. Better still, skim the table of contents, pick an article that seems worth reading, and you're ready to go. And by the way, make me a photocopy so I can read it too, before you and I have a conversation about what you found interesting in the article."

Later, the student joins a literature circle, having selected one from a group of five different novels concerning life in Japan. I am impressed by the chart he presents to his group, listing the differences between the two cultures, his and Japan's. And later we will all view clips from the Tom Cruise film *The Last Samurai*. The literacy modes intersect, and the meaning-making moments grow.

Books and Biscotti

I recently read an article in *The New Yorker* describing a meeting of a book club held at the home of the author of the book the group had read. Everyone met at the townhouse on the Upper West Side, excited about chatting with the author, and proceeded to enjoy the discussion, followed by treats the author had made—chocolate biscotti and home-brewed coffee. While the writer of the article had his tongue firmly planted in his cheek, I could only picture the membership of my own book clubs, much less grand than this, and much more informal, but nonetheless significant.

Ron chats with me over a vegetable burger at a fast food restaurant about religious books he is reading—works examining the life of Jesus, the catacombs of Rome, the history of Egypt; Bob shares his new folklore stories, different versions of tales told before, reworked and rethought from new information and unique perspectives; Larry has the newest picture books and novels for children, spilling out of his office, ready for me to borrow; Shelley stops by my office with three new professional books she has ordered online, and helps me decide which one to read; Linda, over coffee, shares her favourite book set, a thematic collection (always filled with emotional connections) of wonderful resources for children; Joan, over lunch, brings me a new book on anti-bullying programs in which young adolescents care for young babies and, in doing so, alter their lives. Mary emails me articles from newspapers I don't subscribe to, about education and politics...

And the list of the members of my loose-knit book club goes on and on, as does yours. I would like you to notice the members of your book club, to be aware of what each one offers you and the others in the group, to increase the club's membership, whether on a chat line or over a beer or a coffee, to come to understand that each person in some way has become the stories they share, and that as we participate and engage with them, we

87

are allowed entrance into places in their lives—private places, where only trusted members are admitted. Biscotti or no biscotti, we celebrate with them.

One more epiphany: every teacher can belong to a book club; while most formal book clubs are composed of females, every school book club can count male teachers as members. When a teacher reads the same novel as the other members of a literature circle, when he sits among them, when he engages in an honest conversation with them, when he shares his responses to the text as a human being and not just as a teacher, the other members will feel empowered as co-readers; they will begin to dialogue with a strength and depth not previously noted; a true conversation will emerge, and, over time, a trust in the text and in the group will emerge, and literacy will grow for everyone. I have seen it happen. I am not advocating that we suspend teaching, but that we see our role as literacy teacher in a different light; sometimes we should teach from inside the circle, allowing the students to lead in the dance that we have joined. How *real* can you be, while still remaining professional? You will be surprised at how much you will have to say. Remember: as an equal member of the book club rather than the dominant one, you can lead a guided reading session with the next group; with this reading group, you can respond as a reader. (And why not share your equivalent of biscotti with everyone at the last session?)

At one high school, twelve male teachers served as reading mentors for four or five male students each this year, creating a mini book club as they all read the same novel, and then talked about it together.

I need to mention another type of reading club to which many teachers belong—the reading of books and articles about the teaching profession. I have met teachers and principals in dozens of cities who read the same text and gather once a week to discuss the issues and concerns that may affect their schools and their students, and share their responses with each other. Jeannie Wilson, a literacy consultant in Ontario, invited me to visit one such group in her district, a group of teachers who had been reading a book I had written, *Reading and Writing in the Middle Years*. The conversation that took place, the questions they raised, their careful deliberations about ideas raised in the book, the classroom examples that punctuated and illuminated the discussion points, all opened my eyes to the particular context of their school lives, and helped me to understand the culture of their students and how we need to keep reading and talking in order to build better programs. Those teachers were my instructors, and the text was a jumping-off point as they began to shape what changes they could make in their teaching. I want to be a member of these professional book clubs; I want to learn alongside my colleagues, inside our shared experiences. Texts as teachers; teachers as texts. Jeannie is a skilled group leader. Always inside the circle.

One late Friday afternoon, I stumbled upon a chat room on my computer screen: eight educators from different parts of North America were discussing the work of one of my favourite authors for young people—Cynthia Rylant. Due to my inability to hit the right keys in order to join the chat line, all I could do was read it as others talked, and then download the text when they were through. I have read dozens of books about children's literature, some heavy enough to be sold by the pound, but never have I been more engrossed in a professional conversation. The classroom teachers, the college professor, the librarians, brought to the discussion such passion and excitement about learning. They commented, questioned each other, contributed new information about the author's life and work, shared experiences of hearing her speak at conferences, told stories of their students' adventures with her books, read poems and memoirs the children had written from her writings, read bits of reviews and critical responses from journals, and drew from their own personal lives moments that resonated with those pictured by the writer. Never underestimate the power of teachers when they join forces as professionals and construct knowledge together about a topic that they choose and that matters to them. Virtual book clubs: why not?

Has Anyone Seen My Book Report?

I have given up complaining about book reports. It seems that they have become part of education's mandate forever, and nothing will change the lust for them. Perhaps it's because we can count them, check them off, feel good about accomplishing a task, like ironing the laundry. Just as death and taxes are sure things, the book report has become a dirty fact of every child's school life, and little can be done about it. Children hand in these artificial representations of what they think teachers expect, according to some outline passed down over the years that only proves children can complete a task with ritualized behaviour. Many times I have asked audiences of teachers if they ever cheated on book reports, and they all laugh and raise their hands. Then I question them about their own teaching techniques, and almost all admit to assigning book reports to their own students. It is difficult for many teachers to connect their own life experiences with their teaching practice. I am reminded of a sad story recounted by a young teacher about his days in physical education classes, when he had experienced failure and mockery, always last to be selected for a team, living with constant humiliation. His voice betrayed the pain of those classes, but the damage was deeper than I had expected, for he then stated that he followed the same procedures in his own class because, in his words, "children have to learn how to cope." There was not much I could say. The bruises that negative teaching can inflict last longer than the pictures in the yearbook.

Back to the book report. Are there other response activities that might promote literacy and literature in more long-lasting and developmental ways, that might even encourage youngsters to continue reading into adulthood? Watching Laura struggle through *To Kill a Mocking Bird*, chapter by chapter, disliking the experience and the book, hurts my teaching heart. Was it a set of books hiding on the top shelf of the English bookroom that caused the teacher to begin this particular text? Was it the multicultural make-up of the class of students that demanded an in-depth look at the past treatment of minorities? Was it that this book has been and is being taught in every grade ten class in North America as the best representation of the written word that we can pass on to our children? Or was it that the school also had a copy of the film of the book, thus demonstrating how connected and relevant our teaching strategies were? It doesn't matter; Laura missed the book's story and felt no connection to it, but she doggedly wrote a book report and prepared for the test. Is her teacher unaware, overworked, burnt out or lacking in any thoughtful understanding of why we read and how we can help young people learn to read and then want to read? Teaching is always complicated, but when you begin organizing learning events because you don't trust the learners, you will only be able to fulfill the role of warden, and prisoners quickly learn how to subvert the system. Young teachers often explain to me the necessity for the book report, for how else would we find out who hadn't read the required books? The libraries are full of helpful alternatives that might remedy this problem, but they would have to be sought out and read. What if teachers used their own reading to solve the problem of those young people who won't, can't, but might, could read? At the very least, we would all be in the pool, swimming together.

7. View writing as literacy.

Writing: The Other Side of the Literacy Coin

During Education Week, I was asked to read to a group of students from one school district, and when I arrived at the school gymnasium, I found 600 students, kindergarten through twelfth grade, waiting for me. After a first-grade student introduced me, I shared stories and poems that I had collected over the years, all of them written by young students. At the end of my reading, I was thanked by a secondary senior, who I noticed had been standing at the rear of the room with his peers, who were all trying to physically disassociate themselves from the younger crowd. He ambled up to the stage, and began his comments.

"I thought today was going to be a waste of time, but as the speaker read all the stuff from the young kids, I began to remember what I had written all those years ago in elementary school. I was a writer then, with haiku, and stories, and projects. What happened for the last four years? Why did I quit writing? Doesn't high school believe in writing anymore? Mr. Booth, thanks for the memories."

Of course, many high schools do believe in building lots of writing opportunities, and teachers run writing workshops, poetry seminars, scripting sessions, and e-journals, along with their classroom composition activities, but it may be that writing is seen by too many students as compulsory and assessment-based, without any or much opportunity to write what is on their minds, to consider and reflect on what really matters to them. I remember running a poetry competition in the seventies, in which thousands of students submitted entries, and I had to enlist every friend I knew in the reading and assessing of them. But what I remember most are the notes that accompanied so many of them, sadly telling us that they appreciated so much our reading their poems, because teachers had so little time. How can we make time for the different needs of so many youngsters? One English teacher in a suburban high school organized an online poetry anthology. On the Monday of each week, he would post a poem he had written on the website (he was an accomplished poet), and through the week, students would submit their entries, which he would read, and then on Friday he would post the outcome—an anthology of poems, created by the students, for others to read. Teachers all over North America work on similar projects, giving their time and talents to the students, and their contributions remind us that literacy takes many forms, and learners need to be mentored with significant and meaningful meaning-making events.

Years ago, when Dorothy Heathcote, the noted drama educator, was asked to evaluate my graduate thesis for Durham University in England, I was very concerned that I wouldn't measure up to her expectations, and I awaited her official response with a trembling heart. But when I read her careful assessment, one statement stood out, and it has stayed with me for thirty years. She wondered if, had I written my words on plastic film and hung them on a tree, breezes might have caused the pages to overlap, and as the words and sentences intertwined and mingled, whole new thoughts would have emerged, and my ideas would have been transposed and transmuted into ideas I hadn't known I knew.

This metaphor has remained as a guiding principle in my literacy teaching, and by letting the students enter the dialogue

94

and redirect the learning, I have gone on journeys that would have been missing from my careful planning. My original ideas twist and turn in the hands of the youngsters, and together (because I still drive the school bus), we find mysteries and surprises that breathe life into the curriculum events that fill the classroom. Negotiating the curriculum together creates a sense of ownership for both teacher and student. But I have steered the bus in the wrong direction many times, convinced that what I wanted my students to see was what really mattered. I remember in my fifth-grade classroom working with a story titled "Mafatu and the Killer Shark" in their reader, and at last they seemed to be grabbed by a story from this dull anthology. However, time for the reading period had gone by, so I told the students to put away their readers, and we would move into writing. But we didn't write about sharks lurking underwater; we wrote about the autumn leaves we could view from our classrooms—one of those boring bus rides we take with adults who know best.

During my first two years of teaching, I worked with Reg, who followed his textbook, *Using Our Language*, to the nth degree. Since the act of writing was handled in chapter eleven, that was when he taught it, so his students wrote only in the month of March. The rest of the months were devoted to how writing works, but nobody in Reg's class wrote for nine months of the year.

The Unfriendly Letter

Dear Mr. Booth,

I am in first grade. How are you?
How long does it take to write a big story?
Does your hand get tired when you write? Mine does.

Your friend,
Lisa

I have read Lisa's letter to thousands of teachers, because it represents the best in teaching and learning. Here is a six-year-old girl using all of her knowledge and skills to share her life with me through the art of letter-writing.

She locates herself for me: *I am in first grade.*

She connects to my life: *How are you?*

She asks a relevant question that connects to her own life: *How long does it take to write a big story?*

She recognizes the constant struggle of all of us who write: *Does you hand get tired?* (Our children in first grade still write with those huge logs called primary pencils, provided I am sure by the lumber industry, while we adults, with our giant hands, write with tiny silver pens.)

She signs the letter with the emotional immediacy of a six-year-old: *Your friend, Lisa.*

I wish I had received this letter years before I did. It might have altered my teaching far sooner. During my first year of teaching I taught how to write the "friendly letter." (I now wish that time had been spent learning to craft the unfriendly letter—much more useful.) Following a format in that old textbook *Using Our Language*, we had the plan for the lesson carefully laid out. The regular components were there—salutation, etc., but what was missing was any reason for writing such a letter. Each of the forty students in my class addressed their rough drafts to John Smith, and since they didn't know him, they had little to say but the regular perfunctory remarks. Then they rewrote the letter "in good," using in those days a straight pen which had to be dipped in the inkwell after completing two or three letters, followed by the blotting of the writing so that the message would remain intact. (We had ballpoints but they were considered the devil's tool.) I then graded all these letters written to no one, and we mounted them on the bulletin board for parents' night. All this fuss for no reason other than that I told them to do it. No ownership, no message of worth, no learning.

At the same time, there was a young boy in our class in the hospital with leukemia, but we didn't write him any letters. Instead, we wrote to John Smith, but then we didn't even mail those letters to him. Why would we? He didn't exist. Dorothy Heathcote calls these type of exercises "dummy runs," with no inherent value. Why not teach the strategy with some meaningful events that we could share with others in the form of letters, memos or greetings? Why as a young teacher did I not make such a simple connection between skill and content, between artificial and authentic teaching? Why didn't we write letters that someone would actually read, and if the teacher was the only audience for the writing, why didn't my students write to me as a reader and not just a teacher, and why didn't I read their letters as someone interested in what they had to say and not only as a marker who would circle their imperfections?

The children in that school had so many things going on in their lives that I would have benefited from knowing, that in fact I needed to know if I ever wanted to reach them in meaningful and significant ways. I could have read their letters and then helped them to notice how we could change our writing to make it even stronger. Contrast this experience in my teaching life with one I had while teaching a course in Rochester, New York, in the early nineties. As I was working with the teachers in a high school, the bell rang, and dozens of students ran down the halls clutching letters which turned out to be from American soldiers who had been sent to fight in the Gulf War. The senior class had been assigned a project in which each of them was to write to a soldier to support their efforts away from home. Those soldiers had written back, and for many students these were the first letters of significance they had ever received. Their excitement was evidence of the power that lies in learning events that go beyond skill practice into reasons for acquiring those skills. There are many stories of soldiers who kept their war letters forever, tied with a string and placed in a dresser drawer. It seems that men who would never otherwise put pen to paper will pour their hearts out when faced with the loneliness of separation. Why can't we who teach in schools find situations that call for real communication between people, so that the need to write works in favour of those who need to learn is satisfied?

Certainly email has altered our writing habits forever, as millions and millions of people talk to each other over the airwaves with print using computers. Whether we think of email as a phone call or as a letter, we are writing to each other, without benefit of straight pens, ink or blotters, often without revising what we have to say. I wonder if the students I taught forty years ago are computer-literate, if their children are teaching them to connect to the world out there through the magic of the computer. Or are they still scratching away with those damn pens, following carefully the lessons I taught so carelessly?

My cousin in Washington State writes a Christmas newsletter each year, and I look forward to it. He is an ex-military man, and his wife also served in the armed services. I am impressed that it is he in his family who creates the letter. So many men tell me that they don't like writing, even when those same men are involved with reports and memos and emails all day long. Was it the pressure of handwriting failure that turned them away from writing, were the topics too irrelevant, or did we never include the other subjects in school within the writing framework? This man writes, and he talks with such pride about his son, sixteen years old, and the youngest certified master hunter in his state. This father writes with emotion and pride about his son's accomplishments, and I feel so honoured to read his newsletter, and I write about it hoping that one more father or brother or son or husband will suddenly see writing as a means of representing his life for others to share.

When I read some of the newsletter aloud at a conference in a major city, some of the women teachers booed at the reference to hunting. I guess they just eat and wear animals in the city; let's not hear about the youngsters who shoot them. What world are they connecting to when they read the words? Doesn't the child's home culture matter to them? We don't own the students; we make them literate so they can make wise choices—that's our job. Pass the buffalo wings, would you?

I Will Never Learn to Make a Capital "B"

Of course, those children taking calligraphy courses find new and treasured reasons for using nibs and inks, but the formation of the letters of the alphabet using a particular style falls into the category of art and design, and teaches the writer to notice every detail, to build toward uniformity and balance, to create something beautiful. I watched our friend Laura, who was taking such a course at summer school, become an entirely different student when it came to noticing spelling and letter shapes. The arts teach us to attend, to care about our work, to notice aesthetic qualities. I wish I had known this when I taught my years of handwriting lessons, believing at the time in having children complete rows and rows of circles and loops day after day to no avail; their writing seldom altered.

I watched my own son learn to make his letters smaller and smaller until the words from his pen became almost as linear as the flat line on a heart monitor, freed only by the safety offered by the computer, which balances all our writing forms, no matter our limitations of hand/eye co-ordination, and even offers us a hundred fonts to play with. From this expertise, he returned to pen and ink armed with the knowledge that he, too, could communicate in print with whatever medium he chose. He has his own style, which I could distinguish from a hundred other examples; he can return when he chooses to the world of personal handwriting, as a competent and unique writer.

Our student teachers are often assigned handwriting lessons as part of their first practice teaching, and they often have little knowledge of traditional styles of forming letters, both printed and cursive. I like having my student teachers print and write their names on cards I give them, and then we categorize our cards in groupings that reflect similarities in letter formation and style. Many of them had no idea of their own style of handwriting, some could not distinguish between printed and written symbols, and about one-third of them, usually males, had discarded cursive writing and only printed in upper-case letters throughout their university years. It comes as a surprise to many that there are standardized forms of printing and writing that we can share with our students. Of course, many parents judge their children's handwriting as a marker of educational growth, but the popularity of computers will certainly affect the future of handwriting, and If we move its place in school towards requirements of legibility and uniformity, we may remove much of the frustration and waste of time associated with this unfortunate practice. In my second year of teaching, my principal gave me a refillable pen that I could use in my classroom. It leaked, and a black stain appeared on the upper pocket of the first Harris tweed sport jacket I ever purchased. My aunt removed the pocket, cut off the offending stain, and sewed the shortened version back on. From that experience grows my true feeling about the teaching of handwriting, a messy subject at best. Has anyone seen my blotter?

Handwriting is often a struggle for children, leading to frustration and even withdrawal because they cannot represent their thoughts on paper in ways that promote an easy flow of ideas and communication with others. They are defeated by the mechanics. Authorities such as Donald Graves tell us that continuous writing through the years will lead to handwriting improvement, and that maturity will have an effect on how we form our words.

I receive many letters from children and teachers in the schools I have visited. They are usually delightful, and help me come to grips with what I think happened during my time there. But sometimes the letters are written in the children's hands but in the teacher's voice. On one occasion, thirty children wrote me concerning the errors in spelling and punctuation they thought they had spotted in a reader anthology I had edited. Their comments were written in a very nasty tone, arrogant and contemptuous of me and the texts. I wished that they had asked questions instead of writing such diatribes. No one gains from allowing children to respond carelessly and rudely, especially not the children. I attempted to answer each of their issues, which in the end concerned Canadian-American spellings, variations in the use of the colon, and the difficulties with a typo. Then I explained to them the courtesies involved in writing an unfriendly letter, so that their complaints would be acted upon. I took the time to explain the processes involved in creating a book, and explained that I did not do the typesetting myself. It was a strong but, I hope, professional letter, and I trust the children and the teacher learned something about the publishing process. But children need to recognize the art required in writing a friendly letter, and not be required to act as our puppets when we are angry at the world.

What role does emotion play in becoming a literate human? Why have we been so afraid of tapping into this form of intelligence? I remember a writing teacher in New York confessing to me that she hated teaching kids to write, because they only wanted to write about what they cared about. "I don't care what they care about! It doesn't interest me. Just learn the mechanics, for God's sake." It is certainly frustrating to see kids making the same spelling and syntactical mistakes year after year, but having worked for thirty years with teachers taking graduate courses, I'm profoundly aware that we continue to grow as language users forever, and there is always so much more to learn. As I read a thesis or a dissertation, I'm always interested in what the writer has to say, and how he or she has decided to say it. We can work on the bits and pieces of text later, and we will. And if the writers are passionate about their discoveries, and if they are engaged in examining the implications of their findings, and if they give them to me with trembling hands because they care so much about what they have written, then I will read and be involved with both the texts and the writers—"the tale, the teller, the telling, and the told." I appreciate the struggle to capture with print and image what has entered our minds as we assimilate and interpret and represent what we think we have found. We will write our way into literacy.

Think of a school where the students spend a week, or even months, exploring a topic or theme that interests them, as a class, or in groups, or, occasionally, as individuals. What will they read, write, construct, observe, record, paint, revise, make, present? How will we organize their time and help them track their experiences? What resources, including technology, books, magazines, and films, will we search for to deepen their experiences? How will they share and reflect at the close of the inquiry? What will they remember and take home to pin on a wall or put on top of their dresser? How will we account for and represent their learning? How are they employing inside and outside school those literacy strategies we keep talking about? What have we taught them about how literacy works, in all its modes and shapes? Good schools everywhere are looking at all of these components as basic to learning, and literacy education (in its new and wider definition, including writing) is a mainstay of every successful school program.

8. Recognize the ages and stages of individuals

I Won't Read, So Don't Ask Me

Imagine the student who can't "school read"; he can manage simple text messaging, he can circle T or F on a test, understand the sports scores in the newspaper or read a fast food menu, but texts that are lengthy, complex or dense scare him away. And you never get better at anything without practising. Is literacy redeemable for this young man? Where do we begin? Let's look at the educators who work with adult illiterates. How can we learn from their experiences? We can begin by reminding ourselves that texts are multiple and varied, that they take many shapes, and that interest is the imperative that will determine who reads which text.

The Invisible Non-Reader

Laura had figured out how to become invisible during reading class. She became teacher's helper, distributing books, washing paintbrushes, tidying bookshelves. It became a highly developed skill, and she was proficient at disappearing from the skill/drill worksheets and the oral reading circle. But her reading strategies never grew, never deepened, and when she lost her invisibility in grade three, she had fallen behind her friends and needed years to play catch-up, which she finally did, thanks to parents and friends.

Colin simply exhibited difficult behaviours, spending a great deal of time sitting outside the principal's office. Although he was supported by a variety of school assistants, by fifth grade he still couldn't read a simple text, nor could he spell his last name. Fifty years ago, when I was a student in eighth grade, the boys with limited reading skills were allowed to wash the principal's car, flood the skating rink or assist the caretaker, all in the hopes of missing reading period. The text selections were too difficult, held little interest for them, and interfered with their dreams of leaving school at sixteen. And yet, in this new century, we find so many students unable to process the texts of their school lives. About 25 percent of them fail the literacy exit test written in grade ten. Are we just too understaffed to offer them successful remediation in reading and writing? Or have they just maintained that invisibility factor?

I have just participated in a literacy conference at which I had the opportunity to listen to a talk by Jacques Demers, who coached the Montreal Canadiens to the Stanley Cup in 1993 and was later a general manager in the NHL. He admits that he is illiterate. "I could read a little bit but I can't write very well. I took to protecting myself. You put a wall around yourself. And when I was given the possibility of talking, I could speak well and I think that really saved me."

He told us that his inability to read and write was the result of an abusive and impoverished childhood.

"The other thing I wanted to say was that if I could not write or read, it was because I had so much of a problem with anxiety because of the things going on in the family. I couldn't go to sleep at night. I'd go to school and I couldn't learn anything."

Since leaving he NHL coaching ranks, Demers has worked as a hockey analyst at the French-language RDS network.

He is happy that he has gone public about his illiteracy, and I know that his story will help make all of us more aware that literacy learning is a complicated process, intertwined with all of our life experiences. We will watch for those children blocked by pain, and we will help them become readers and writers. And we have Jacques Demers, among others, to thank for their courage.

Some of us become readers at twenty-one, thirty-one or even fifty-one. But perhaps we need to define our terms more carefully. What does "illiterate" mean in the twenty-first century? I cannot read efficiently so many different texts—manuals, schedules, guitar magazines, sheet music, and almost anything with numbers in it. Are we using inappropriate texts with our students? Are we beginning formal literacy teaching too early? Are we so bothered by their disruptive behaviours that we ignore the miscreants? Are we losing too many boys and many girls because of our poor choices of suitable texts? Do we assess and then not use the information to build our teaching methodologies? Are there not enough support personnel to help us? Are government curricula too rigid, too complex, and too many?

After talking to parents in a small town, I stopped at the local fast food chain, and asked the young girl behind the counter for a bowl of chili. It was after 9:00 p.m., and she said the chili was pretty well finished, but she could scrape up a bowl. She wasn't making eye contact with me, and I began to chat about her schooling. She was sixteen, had quit school, and this was her first job. She was looking at me now, and said that there were some hot biscuits in the back. I ate them with my chili, and realized that it takes so little to offer respect to a young woman who has been relegated to such a limited literacy culture. There are schools now where she would thrive, and find hidden strengths and talents. After, she might choose to go back to working in the restaurant, but it would be because she wanted to.

When I was a child, my newspaper comic section included "Invisible Scarlet O'Neil," who could squeeze her wrist and become invisible in order to fight crime. What I thought to be an imaginary trick has become truth for too many youngsters; they have opted for hiding in the shadows, or sometimes being herded together in a gymnasium by the dozens, all of them knowing why they have been sent there, feeling hopeless, marked by their inabilities, leftovers from the blue-jay group of yesteryear, squeezing their wrists and hoping for an ectoplasmic miracle.

Boys Will Be Boys, and Girls Will Be Readers

The norms of gender change constantly. I was extremely surprised one winter to see my son's entire hockey team dye their hair blond. While this may seem a trivial indication of change to some, for some boys I taught in the sixties, having long hair like the Beatles' forced them to leave their homes.

If reading is about the interaction between reader and text, if making sense of print demands background that can shape our interpretations and understanding and connect us to the author's intent and words, why should gender not be considered a significant factor, along with social status, age, ethnicity, subculture, and even the mood and purpose of the person reading? We bring everything we are to a text, and being a boy is part of how males' out-of-school literacy practices often go unrecognized or, more important, untapped in the classroom. What many boys value as literacy texts can unintentionally be dismissed or demeaned in school. And yet their deep involvement in and dedication to computers, magazines, CD-Roms, videos, card collections, and hobbies can offer us entry points into their lives as readers and writers.

Of course, children are decoding gender long before they are decoding print. They build up their concepts of gender right from birth, depending on whether they are girls or boys, and it is certainly a key issue by three or four years of age. And how does this happen? How do individuals acquire gender? There are many theories, but none seems to help us fully understand this complex defining process. Nonetheless, very young children notice and respond to visible differences between boys and girls, and some recognize that these gender differences are fundamental to their lives and to how they will interact in society. Nature and nurture have become catch words, but how the brain thinks, how the unconscious works, how the affective and emotional factors relate, how the child is raised (both intentionally and unintentionally), how the social structures surround the child–all of these factors contribute to the child's perception of gender.

One of the great appeals of computers today for boys is that they are intrinsically motivating and students can set their own goals. It is easy for us, as educators, to forget how rapidly computers and technology have become a part of the repertoire of tools available to us in our schools, and equally easy to forget the benefits these tools are able to provide. For many boys, who may have a natural predilection for solitary, fact-based activities, computer use is a natural and comfortable tool for learning. However, at the same time, computers can prove to be an obstacle for them in their literacy learning, given that information on the web is frequently a bit inaccurate and at times incorrect.

We know from research on gender and literacy that boys often prefer resources (books, magazines, websites) that favour facts over fiction. What does this mean for their future literacy abilities? Will fictional stories exist for them?

In a recent column in the *Globe and Mail* entitled "Why There's No Beer at the Book Club," critic Kate Taylor examined the reasons why most novels are marketed to and bought by women. Women read far more than men; they have for the last three centuries. We know this today through our own observations at home and at school, and from publishers and polls. Some educators blame ths phenomenon for the reason boys are lagging (somewhat) behind the girls on literacy tests. The traditional excuses for this disparity often focus on the needs for males to identify with the protagonist, while women read about characters different from themselves, empathizing with the fictional people because of their emotional strengths. Of course men read, but they usually choose non-fiction, history, finance, and sports. Should they read more fiction? It depends on the type of books men want and need, and their reasons for reading them. But school can open up new areas of novel literature that boys are not aware of, and school culture can offer boys safe havens for reading novels that may be seen as a female activity outside in the mainstream culture.

When I began researching material about boys and literacy, I was amazed at the quantity of available resources for parents and teachers, especially on the internet. People are certainly concerned about males and literacy. Dozens of books have been published in the last few years documenting issues in male culture and in raising and schooling boys. Some emphasize biological differences between males and females; others take a sociological approach; still others struggle for a culturally elitist model promoting literary wonders. Personally, I need to look at them all to find directions for supporting parents and teachers and educational policy-makers, but especially for helping youngsters themselves begin to take control of their literacy lives, aware of their needs and interests as developing readers and writers.

Before deciding on plans of action, we need to examine the issues pertaining to the literacy lives of boys, how they perceive themselves as readers, and how parents, teachers, and peers influence their literacy development. The role of gender in reading success is complex, and I want to explore many of the assumptions and stereotypes that parents and educators have about boys and how they handle the world of print text. We need to listen to the voices of writers for young people, of authorities in this field, and, most important, of boys and men as they reveal their literacy challenges, struggles, tastes, and values, and offer us insights into how we can support all learners in their literacy journeys.

If we believe that all children should have access to the literacy world, how will we ensure that boys, in particular, see themselves as readers who can handle the requirements of a variety of texts? Non-readers tell us stories of punishment and pain, of no care and no touch, a world where books never metamorphosed into friendly objects, where worksheets and controlled readers dictated their eye movements and caused their reading hearts to beat irregularly. They drown in printer's ink.

We know that no single category includes all boys or all girls. We don't need to add to the stereotype of classifying all boys' behaviours, tastes, and attitudes into one single frame, nor do we want to reinforce the generalizations that are often applied to boys. But as we look at studies and reports that examine boys and girls and their learning styles and special interests, their growth patterns and their stages of intellectual development, we do notice differences. These differences are not in all boys or all girls, but in enough of them to cause us to reflect about our demands on their young lives.

There are definite problems with the ways in which many boys view themselves as literate beings, with how they approach the acts of reading and writing, and with how they respond to assessments of their skills. At least the faltering test scores have opened up discussion on these issues that concern many teachers and parents.

How closely are we watching and interpreting the alarmist data? Are *all* boys at risk? If not, which ones? How significant are developmental stages in boys' literacy abilities? What is "normal" literacy achievement for a six-year-old boy? Is it the same for a six-year-old girl? Which boy and which girl? Are we concerned about the girls who are doing poorly? And most important, what do we mean by "literacy"? How we as parents and as educators consider these questions will determine our school policies and curriculum, but how we answer them will determine the future of our children.

At the end of every talk I give, parents and teachers line up to ask me questions, and they are almost always about boys in literacy trouble: they don't read, can't read, won't read, don't write, can't write, can't spell. Those of us who are responsible for educating boys are deeply concerned over the plight of many of them who can't or won't enter the literacy club at school. But our rules for school entry are very strict, and oddly enough, computer skills and other forms of "unorthodox" reading are seldom part of the qualifications. In fact, many boys have joined alternate literacy clubs, just not the one we'd hoped they would.

Wrestling with Ideas

As a boy, I was a huge fan of professional wrestling. My guys were The Sheik and Bobo Brazil. The only way I could find out about these wrestlers was through the newsstand wrestling magazines.

So I'm at the library, and I see a whole shelf of different magazines. As I go to check out my books, I summon up all my courage and ask the librarian if the library has any wrestling magazines. That was what I thought I had asked; instead I think I asked her to show me what her face would look like if she sucked on a lemon for a hundred years. She looked as if she was about to

faint at the mere mention of wrestling magazines in her library. She made me feel stupid and I never went back.
—Patrick Jones, *Wrestling with Reading*

A few months ago, I spent two hours sitting in a school library engaged in a lengthy conversation with seven ninth-grade boys chosen by their English teacher because of their limited literacy competencies. Since I had been invited to speak to parents and teachers in this island community about boys and literacy the next day, the organizer felt that it might be helpful to spend some time with students from one of their schools, chatting about their views on how they were growing as readers and writers. Their teacher, a mature educator, aware of their print phobias and difficulties, ushered them into the room with supportive and comforting words.

As we began the conversation with introductions, they wanted to know who I was and why I was there, what I expected, and what I would do with what they had to say. When I explained that I needed to meet some young men from this school district to explain how reading was being taught, they laughed and shouted that they were the worst readers in the class. Like all students meeting a new and untested teacher, they began the session by teasing each other, laughing at every comment, talking over each other, until they began to discover that I was actually listening to them, rephrasing and commenting on each of their statements. I love that moment in teaching when the group coalesces, when the members begin to accept the dynamic of the event and act as legitimate participants. Their body positions change, their faces light up, their conversations deepen. The clown stops grinning, and the shy one laughs.

I focus my responses and comments with as much strength as I can muster, and I try to keep eye contact with each speaker while he is talking, no matter what is happening around us. I try to reflect back to each boy what I think he has said, and I attempt to involve everyone as much as possible. I suspend judgment; I offer anecdotes from my own life and my son's life; I redirect when comments become too personal or seem off-track; I sometimes fail to respond in the most enabling manner, but I push on, as I would with any group. Conversation is never smooth, never without false starts and off-topic wanderings.

The boys began to list what they had read during the past week of their lives. My goal was to help them see that they were indeed readers, that their self-described illiteracy was a mislabelling of their true reading behaviours, and that there were types of texts they could handle which I could not. And they came through with TV guides, newspaper sports pages, emails, chat lines, math texts, car magazines, a novel about Terry Fox, and then—with complete consensus—wrestling magazines. One boy subscribed to two magazines and described the different features of each, in style and content. As a group, we carried on an animated conversation concerning the inherent values and contradictions of this genre, and wrapped our minds around the issue of sports vs. entertainment, and where wrestling fit on the continuum. The group decided to place it higher than ice dancing and lower than synchronized swimming. Then one young man took from his jeans pocket a carefully folded, legal school contract concerning his joining the wrestling team. He read it aloud, and others informed me that it required a parent's signature if the student was under fourteen (their smiles indicated that none was in this particular group). Others explained that the contract was established in order to prevent parents from suing the school board if there were to be a physical injury. Four boys were signing up today. Wrestling matters.

I asked tough questions in our conversation because I wanted to honour these students, but my queries often grew

112

from their own comments, and I tried to respect their participation with my own commitment to listen to what they had to say. We were involved in an actual conversation, and I was a contributing member. For real.

When our time was over, I asked the boys if they would take some time that night to rethink their self-labels as non-readers, shook each of their hands, and left them to enjoy the pizzas their teacher had ordered as a reward for putting up with the ordeal. But the next day, I talked about these lads in my speech to the town, because I had felt so strengthened by the stories of the literacy lives of their boys, sharing our brief time together with the parents, the teachers, the administrators, the politicians, and other members of the community who had wanted to know about boys and literacy, but especially how their boys were entering the literacy club.

I want to mention one boy who had described his major literacy event of the week, an email from his father in prison who was being released to a half-way house the next week. His story reminds us that the lives of many of the young people in our care are complex and often full of pain and turmoil; literacy is about the communication between writer and reader, and sometimes the event is too intense, too personal, to discuss. All I am certain of is that that young man is a reader, and his father is a writer.

9. Explore how words work.

Stick-handling through the Words

I'm asked again and again, "What about spelling?" or "What about grammar?" Why would these literacy attributes not be part of our teaching if we want our students to have the widest range of tools to draw from as readers and writers? But how do we give students these bits and pieces of language knowledge alongside honest, significant literacy experiences? Just getting ready to read and write for twelve years won't work.

I remember a well-known columnist ranting on about the necessity for skill and drill. His two examples revealed his lack of insight into how children learn; he revelled in Wayne Gretzky's story of how he practiced at 5:00 in the morning on a backyard rink in 10-below temperatures. The difference between Wayne and the fourth-grade kid working on his two hours of drill sheets seems so obvious: Wayne was wearing skates and moving about on ice with a stick in his hand, knowing that he was gaining the hockey skills every day that he would use in achieving his future dream. Would the child in school be as lucky as to know his future at twelve years of age? How do we build a rink for readers and writers, so they can be at one with the learning and experience? Will Wayne's father cheer on the boy with the workbook whose skates are in the classroom? Skill is acquired through constant effort. But we need to know where the path leads.

My son attended hockey school for three summers, and then a full year for his last two terms of high school. I had observed him for all those years, growing stronger and faster, acquiring those goalie strategies and techniques, and dreaming of the NHL, as all other players on teenage teams are wont to do. His room at home was full of Patrick Roi photos and pennants and trophies, and hockey school offered him a chance to practise his love and complete his academic subjects. So he went away for a year, and weekend visits were our family times.

What a year! Practice from 6:30 a.m. to noon, school work 1:00 to 5:00, hockey from 6:00 to 9:00 p.m. Games on weekends. How hard young people work when their wants match their needs! I yearn for schools that offer youngsters a range of activities to grow through. I know that many schools and teachers are finding ways of offering students so much more than I experienced, but then I was a child of school. What about those who weren't, who found school a foreign place, who never understood the immigration laws of entering, who never had their school passports stamped. My heart aches for the ones we missed, who live outside the moat, and sometimes throw rocks at us. I celebrate the music class's trip across the country to compete at a national conference, but I would be ecstatic to see the shop class touring another city to see changes in technology and industry. What would those kids read and write to prepare to participate as valued guests, to share with the school on their return?

Hockey skates for all, I say!

Parsing Our Way into Oblivion

I remember a conference speaker using this example of the gap between skill and connection: "Bill broke his arm." Student responses included:

Oh no! Where did he break it—in one or more places?

116

What was ER like?
Did he have medical insurance?
Will it affect his work?
He wasn't a musician, was he?

And so on. One simple sentence from a grammar exercise reveals the complexities of language, how it sets off chain reactions as we are driven by the imperative to make meaning. It is interesting to note that we never use real text to analyze in grammar exercises: it would be too difficult, too complex. Let's just say Bill broke his arm, underline the verb, and move on.

For years, puzzles and word games have taught us about language. Now, with computer websites, opportunities for language play are plentiful. My son and his grandmother used to buy big books of word puzzles on holidays and found great pleasure in the challenge, while I, who can parse a sentence with the best of them, stuck to mystery novels. I do remember a holiday in Maine when ten of us played the board game Balderdash, making up imaginary definitions, helping the young ones enter the contest and laughing at the wacky attempts of the rest of us. Do all children have memories of the pleasure and puzzlement of language games? The more we know about how language works, the more we can work the language. I have given up on telling students that "For you and I" should be "For you and me," since almost all of my colleagues use "I" now. Perhaps we will accept it as an idiom. My son learned a trick: if you drop the "you," then "for I" sounds strange. In giving a talk now, I have to explain my choice of 'me," not "I," but then language has always changed and will continue to change. Fun to know why, though.

I have a friend who loves to harangue an audience about the lack of grammar in schools. I often count his syntactical errors but say nothing—unusual for me, to say the least. And of course "ain't" is in the dictionary.

We need to know how to talk about our language, and labels such as noun and verb serve us well. But verb endings, subject verb agreement, and tense misuse all need to be discussed as students grow into literacy adulthood. We need to know the stages of language knowledge, and not waste any student's time on grammar worksheets that have little or no effect on how they speak or write. Knowing when to use appropriate language patterns is a skill; knowing why is a gift. I am saddened by "seen" and "have went" and "done" used inappropriately, but I say, "It's me," when I say hello on the phone.

Use the grammar worksheets, but make certain there is carry-over into the students' lives, not to mention your own. Give them language options that will enrich their lives, all the while recognizing that cultural variants often hold the most meaning.

The Phonics War

My son and I used to have the unfortunate opportunity of listening to different talk radio programs on our drive to see Grandma in Florida, and he was more than surprised to hear the political vitriol of the hosts and guests. But one caller I remember was a woman defending the teaching of phonics; she truly believed that no one else on the continent was doing as effective a job as she was in drilling those nuts and bolts of literacy into the children's psyches, and she explained that her philosophy and pedagogy were given to her by her grandmother and her mother, both teachers, who had acquired the truth of the phonics cure for non-readers a century ago, and had passed on the worksheets to the next generation of teachers. As she said, "Why would we exchange a sure-fire method of becoming literate for liberal gobbledy-goop?" She saw phonics instruction as an end in itself, not as a support for readers who wanted or needed to make meaning with a particular text. For her, there was no time to waste on reading until they could "decode." Cracking codes instead of constructing meanings. "Children should spend their time on the sub-skills of reading rather than actually reading." "Mark those worksheets. Demand corrections. Never let a story get in the way of the learning." And what happens to those generations of students living out their literacy lives; what texts do they read and write; have they benefited as literate citizens from the teaching they encountered? Did school matter? And why do some educational groups attempt to hijack phonics, as if the rest of us have made a pact with the devil to do away with giving children knowledge about words? To the proficient reader, phonics is usually irrelevant. But with beginning readers, we need to find ways of letting them in on the secrets so they can discover that this process called reading is worth acquiring. And we can't let a day go by without experiencing real reading events alongside whatever sound/letter activities we think necessary. To those bullies who rant against real reading and attack those of us who advocate it as "liberal phonics haters," I can only say, give me back my phonics teaching! I love exploring how words work! Didn't you learn to share in kindergarten?

There never was a phonics war. Different groups have tried to marginalize each other's positions in the teaching of reading by using labels and name-calling in an attempt to influence reading curriculum, and this debate will continue forever, since it is based on ideology. The term "balanced literacy" was developed to articulate specific strategies for acquiring word knowledge that would be a significant component of all school literacy programs. Even this did not placate certain groups who believe in *phonics* first and foremost. These groups are often aligned with right-wing fundamentalist groups, who for decades have attacked *whole word* teaching, instead of *phonics drill.* But even the most conservative authorities writing on the issue suggest that we embed the *word study* inside authentic, real text for the reader. The only reason to learn about the relationship between how we speak and how we represent speech is so that we can read and write more effectively. There are some proponents of an *intense phonics program* who feel we should only teach about words, never actually use them or see them used in texts that hold meaning. As a teacher and a reader, I value word knowledge, and today there are very fine books and papers to help us learn as teachers how to assist young readers in acquiring literacy strategies; word recognition, word constructing, and word-solving are vital processes in interacting with a text. But the goal is to read with as much understanding as possible. I weep for the children who never get to practise reading, to enjoy, learn from, and celebrate different text modes in school; they are too often fooling with the nuts and bolts of literacy that never seem to fit the literacy machine.

All wars are destructive; so many innocent people suffer. It's time we declared an armistice.

The Writing on the Living-Room Wall

When I arrived to pick up my son at the sitter's home one evening, he was sitting on the couch with the sitter's younger daughter, both of them staring into space. I subsequently learned that Laura and her mom and dad had been attempting to get her to complete her homework in first grade—sight recognition of ten words that she just couldn't seem to remember. After a futile hour and a half, Mom was upstairs crying. Dad had retreated to the basement, and the children were staring straight ahead. I took down the ten words that had been taped to the living-room wall, found some blank file cards, and asked Laura to tell me ten words that she could read, and I wrote them on the cards.

Fluffy – the cat
Jay – her friend

And so on. I taped the cards to the wall, and I said she had finished her homework. Learning to read must not be painful. No one I know seeks out painful experiences. Why would we want to engage in activities in life that we remember with such sadness and regret? What is the slogan "Learning for life" supposed to mean? We avoid what makes us sad, or we blot it out.

Ms. Moffett Is Fragile Today

Abby Goodnough, a reporter for the *New York Times*, spent a year observing a new teacher, Ms. Moffett, in the New York education system. As an outsider, her observations and perceptions in her book, *Ms. Moffett's First Year: Becoming a Teacher in America*, illuminate so clearly the issues that confront every new teacher, the administration, and the children. Ms. Moffett was part of a program in which uncertified teachers with excellent backgrounds were permitted to teach without having taken an educational degree. They would teach a class under the stewardship of a master teacher, take evening and summer courses, and then be granted a teaching certificate. Ms. Moffett was one of these teachers.

One interesting aspect of the story is the problem of how Ms. Moffett would handle the literacy program, a very regimented, controlled, step-by-step series of lessons that the administration would monitor very closely, which they indeed did. The tension arose over the teacher's tendency to become involved in the direction the students would lead in after reading a story in their books, taking time away from the lesson plan to be followed. My heart went out to this teacher, who, lacking so many of the traditional skills and strategies of the experienced teacher, faced undisciplined, unmanaged children each morning, always with a smile, until the ship would begin to sink. Admonished again and again by the supervising staff, she would struggle to stay on course, but always become diverted by the children's interests and questions.

The reporter was very astute with her interpretation of what was happening, trying in her own mind to reconcile the two directions, feeling strongly that the children required a careful sequence of lessons, yet recognizing the organic nature of children's learning. Ms. Moffett persevered, remained in teaching, and grew as a professional. The question of balance remains. How much directed teaching; how much child-directed learning? What is happening in literacy teaching is a blended program, where we as instructors are clear about the strategies we want youngsters to become proficient in, while selecting and allowing children to self-select the texts they will want to read, the texts that will be significant in their lives.

Some school districts, like Ms. Moffett's, demand that teachers follow a predetermined script when they work with a student on a literacy selection. How limiting a strategy is this for teachers and students? When is a directed script useful in teaching literacy? After all, as adults we follow instructions and recipes and manuals carefully in so many reading experiences. We take our students step by step through a test procedure; we follow a scientific experiment without deviating from the directions. I think it can offer support to a teacher to have a map of the territory, an outline of what another educator or team considers significant in promoting literacy growth among students. But when the teacher feels a degree of confidence with a text, that script can act as a resource or stimulus for an interactive discussion with students, one in which they can take the lead in exploring the text while the teacher follows them, nudging and mentoring them into a more intensive reading of the selection, moving them further along the continuum of thoughtful learning than they were expected to go.

My heart aches when I witness extreme differences between two classrooms in one school. In the literacy-rich space, students read a variety of texts in a variety of modes; they explore the literature of their home culture; they act on their curiosity and

122

wonder; they deepen their potential as literate citizens; they are encouraged to employ their imaginations in all aspects of learning; they often find school full of joyful and satisfying literacy events; they seldom experience a day of drudgery, punishment or low-level, non-involving, repetitive activities; they know they are growing as readers and writers and know what to do to continue towards proficiency. In the literacy-impoverished classroom, the children are always preparing to read and write, seldom actually engaged in interpreting and constructing meaning. They are often hungry for story.

I want to know how words work so that I can write my thoughts more clearly and communicate them more effectively, and I have come to love the power of language; I notice how speech sounds connect to written words (loosely defined as phonics) so that I can make sense of what the text is saying to me, so that I can wonder about it, reflect on it, and challenge it. I use my word knowledge to read something that matters to me. What other possible reasons would we have for teaching phonics?

I like the philosophy of the well-known children's author and educator Mem Fox, who follows the three secrets of reading: understanding the world (general knowledge, conversations, life experiences), knowing how language works (all about books, the internet, newspapers, advertisements), and seeing how print works (letters, meanings, upper and lower case, punctuation).

She says that good readers use the three secrets "simultaneously, rapidly and efficiently." Do you think that disabled readers became lost inside one of the secrets of reading, unable to weave the three parts together? Did they not have enough information to bring to the text? Did they not understand the value of the text? Were they stymied by too many words they had to attack with their own limited knowledge of phonics?

Did the whole daily reading experience just end in frustration and a sense of failure?

Those who work with adult illiterates tell us that they need the three components—the three secrets of reading—in their efforts to help these mature struggling readers, and they usually begin their sessions with, "What would you like to read about?" Makes sense to me.

Does Spelling Count?

As Winnie the Pooh said, "I am a bear of very little brain, and long words bother me." My exact feelings, especially when I am writing those words down and having difficulty with their spelling, as does everyone, at some time, even those among us who decry the present condition of teaching of spelling in our schools. Like Pooh Bear, I need help with those special words that wiggle and waver in the heat of writing. I have learned to leave their print representation for the moment and to go on putting down my ideas, returning later to worry over them and to seek help from friends and other resources. But for many people, especially children, spelling is such a great problem that they avoid writing, use simple words, take far too long pondering or give up caring in frustration. Almost everyone I meet apologizes for his or her lack of spelling strengths, and yet I live in a world of academics, writers, and publishers! What lies behind our difficulties with spelling much of the English language, and what attitudes and disabilities are we passing on to our students? We seem to have reached an impasse in even discussing spelling with teachers and parents at loggerheads over expectations, with children either being drilled or ignored as developing spellers. Teachers have actually said to me, "I teach spelling, but please don't tell the consultant because we're not supposed to."

No subject in education seems to cause more grief than spelling, even today, with computer spell checks, spelling machines, and invented spelling. If I address parents, you can rest assured that, no matter the topic, spelling concerns will be among their questions. And they are honest concerns, full of past resentments, present frustrations, and future fears for their children. And like all questions relating to children, they cannot be answered simply. For there is no program, no book, no speller, no machine that alone will build language competence in a child. Unfortunately, spelling can't be isolated from our language processes, from attitudes to reading and writing, from homes where print power is seen as valuable, or from classrooms where words are recognized as treasures, and where teachers act as guides to that wealth rather than wardens who keep it for themselves. Spelling wardens. We should give them uniforms and billy clubs. For a child trained over the years with negative spelling teaching, there is little hope of recovering, little chance of becoming "word struck," a lover of language, a writer eager and anxious to find and try new words to make subtle meanings, to paint images with print.

Spelling in English is a complex act, representing hundreds of years of changing styles and words from dozens of languages with different orthographies. Those adults who have an extensive vocabulary, write frequently, and have facility in spelling are the very ones who surround themselves with dictionaries of all types, wordlists, and thesauruses, who use mnemonics for those odd words, who notice origins and derivations, who read newspaper columns on contemporary word use, who are not afraid of poems, who can do cryptic crosswords, and who engage in word play. And those who didn't pass those old spelling tests seldom know the tricks, the support texts or the techniques for spelling. We fail them all the way to the grave.

As always in education, any change is initially suspect. The agents of change become martyrs to their cause, or those to be changed resist through fear or ignorance or stubbornness, and the children wander wearily through years of language arts, never knowing what will be expected of their spelling from year to year, constantly asking the question, to no one in particular, "Does spelling count?"

Well, of course, it counts, but not as a grade on a paper. In the past many teachers, myself included, taught spelling as a testing process, with no regard for the developmental backgrounds of the different children who would be writing the same word. Punishment and humiliation were the order of the day. Poor spellers received a zero on their papers every Friday for eight years, seldom garnering any strategies or techniques for becoming independent writers. Words were circled, usually in red, with the strange figure of four marks being deducted for each misspelling from the total of twenty-five. Teachers stuck to their guns, and principals would even dictate the words over the public address system, enthralled with their power to instill in students the fear of writing down a single little word in English. Parents would panic over the test scores and replace reading time at home with drill time for spelling. The cycle never altered from year to year, grade to grade. When I asked a colleague why she publicly displayed the spelling grades of all her students on the classroom wall throughout the year, her answer reeked of moralistic retribution for the sin of "lack of effort." She felt all children could spell all words if they just worked hard enough. She completely disregarded age, competence, background, context, and development. She ruled by the test and rewarded by the chart. She was twenty-one. This teacher had never read a paper on spelling, never mind a book on language development in children, the history of the teaching of spelling, the feelings and attitudes of children being taught spelling, or the development of the spelling text. (But then, I have seldom met a teacher of formal spelling lessons who knew anything about the authors or the validity of the spelling books they were using, books that often decided the fate of a child.) Teaching knowledge and practice were based solely on how the teacher had been taught or, even more sadly, on how she thought she had been taught. Is there a teacher among us who did not begin a career by emulating those memories of control at the front of the classroom? And were our images clouded by our insecurities or inability to achieve those expected states of perfection? Were we struggling to have a chance to redeem ourselves, to prove our worth by pouncing on the tiniest error of a child who was trying to make sense of our complex code? I am certain that I was. I taught from a speller, 9:20 a.m. to 9:40 a.m. each and every day, and I tested those words on Friday. I circled them on Saturday and returned them on Monday. A meaningless ritual, but I felt competent and righteous. I was nineteen.

What changes us as teachers? What alters our perceptions of what we are trying to achieve with children? When a consultant mentioned to me that spelling was a visual problem, that we try to see the word in our minds, I was instantly aware of the problem with the venerated spelling bee. Why didn't we let the children write the words down? Every one of us knows that is exactly what we do when we are asked to spell a word. We have to see it, change it, look at it again, and match it to the patterns we have noticed over the course of our reading/writing lives. And did we give these children who couldn't spell a buddy, a partner, a group to collaborate with against those demons of orthography, so that they too became part of the meaning-making process? What has caused this new fascination with spelling bees on film and television? Those few children with enormous memories for unused words make life so painful for the rest of us who may struggle to remember when *i* comes before *e,* if indeed it does.

Still, I worry about authorities who tell us that computers will spell for us, that we will have no need to know how to spell. Of course they are reacting against the years of torment and failure that so many students have had to endure in the name of learning to spell, and I, too, want to wipe that from the classroom slate. But the spelling of a word is a special thing. It is a record of the origins of our language, a recognition of a symbol system that has grown over centuries, so that we can communicate to each other not only ideas but the layers of history and meaning behind those ideas. As we learn about words, we are making thoughtful connections, careful decisions, and caring contributions to collaborative sharing. In Japan I have watched calligraphy competitions, where the paper, the ink, the letters, and the flow all add to the aesthetic power of the writing, I want to inspire in children a similar passion for words, so that spelling will be a part of the whole of language.

My son used a speller in grade four. He used an old, traditional speller and endured pre-tests and final tests for wordlists. When we talked about his miscues, he treated them as jigsaw puzzles not yet complete, but he was still ready to have a go. There was no fear, no humiliation. His teacher worked with words as he did with everything—with energy, commitment, and love. He played the cello while my son worked with the wordlist, and somehow that classroom situation was context enough for learning. I delighted in Jay's spelling attempts, his anger over words that shouldn't be spelled "that way," his joy over succeeding in approximating a new word. Jay loved puns and riddles and songs and reading and games and commercials. He became word conscious, word struck. The spelling text didn't seem to hurt.

As a very young and inexperienced teacher, I visited an aunt one weekend when I was ill with the flu. She and her friend Thelma marked my grade five spelling tests for me. Such a relief. They had many laughs over the spelling miscues of my grade five students, but when I returned the papers to the children a great commotion arose and they complained loudly that many words had been overlooked, and others wrongly circled. My markers had missed the boat. But because they had done so the children had noticed their words more carefully than at any time before. They felt injustice, and they wanted action. My aunt and Thelma were removed as markers (red-faced) and I never again gave a spelling test in that manner. It seemed so pointless.

As a student in grade eight, I was a perfect speller on tests, except for one error that year—the word "separate." I was mortified: and wrote it out a hundred times. But on the final year-end test, I misspelled it again. My terror had blocked my reason. Today, I struggle with spelling—so many words to use, so little time to reflect. But I have broken the barriers, and I seek out new words and new ways to use them. I know how to help myself, how to edit and revise. Words are my lifeblood now. I revel in the *New Yorker*'s lack of typos; I collect every word play book written for children; I attempt to write poems. I am afraid of no print.

When my Aunt Marnie wrote letters to me, I never checked her spelling. I read every word, sensed the love and caring behind it, and saved the letters. I know when spelling counts.

How Should We Teach Spelling?

Can we teach spelling in a humane, meaningful, and pedagogically sound manner? Can we become informed teachers whose teaching practice is built on a wide background of solid professional research and information? Do most of us teach the way we were taught, believing that God has chosen the words on the spelling list, and only drill and pain and repetition will assist us in developing children as spellers? We are certainly not all created equal when it comes to spelling, but the red pen, the marks list, the spelling bee, the work books, and the test scores spare no one. Many children have learned to be afraid of words, of reading them aloud, writing them down or using them in stories. As teachers we should rejoice in their attempts to master their code, celebrating their humble efforts, building on the beginning patterns of understanding print processes, and collaborating with the children as they develop as language users. We learn to spell by hypothesizing about the word, testing our letter memory, confirming and modifying our initial attempts. We know that spelling is a developmental process and that negative feedback on our attempts to invent spellings tells us that we can't learn to spell. When children (and adults for that matter) are writing, focusing on spelling correctness during the composing stage will limit ideas and thwart the act of composing. First-draft perfect spelling is an oxymoron for most people.

A very present danger in confronting the difficulties of teaching spelling is that we will give up in despair and retreat from helping children, using such defensive statements as "You can't teach children to spell—either they're spellers or they're not," or "My jurisdiction has forbidden spelling books, and if they don't care, I don't care," or "Why bother, if they'll all use spell checks on their computers when they need to spell a word?" I'm as guilty of these thoughts as any teacher. When, as a young language arts consultant, I ran a workshop on spelling, I received a call the following day from the principal of one of the teachers in attendance, complaining about that teacher's actions which he felt were motivated by my flippant suggestion that we educators should throw the spellers out the window. In fact, that was exactly what that young teacher had his students do. The parents complained, the principal reacted, and I had to explain my comments. Perhaps the teacher was making a point or mocking my ideas or rebelling against the principal; I really don't know. But when the state of California banned spelling texts, that story from my youth came floating back, and I realize that now I want to find all the books I can about spelling, including those damnable spellers. Inside those pages, we can find information about words, buried beneath boring drill, but there nevertheless. The children, alongside the teacher, can ferret out the useful bits, build their own reference points for learning to spell, make games and puzzles that draw our attention to how words work. Where are those texts? I will begin by using them with my son, just as I want him to have as many poetry anthologies as possible so that he can choose those poems that have significance for him.

How can we develop in children an effective visual coding mechanism for spelling? For those for whom this feat remains unaccomplished, how can we support them in their need to function as spellers in society?

My class of student teachers last year were vocal in their descriptions of themselves as poor spellers, and unaware of any strategies or techniques for helping themselves (or their students) to become better spellers. What an opportunity we have for developing young teachers as spelling mentors, for sending into the schools adults who are equipped with background and strategies for promoting word awareness. Spelling is only one aspect of word power. It belongs in the study and use of language by all learners. We will never know how to spell all words. We will never know all about all words. We continue to grow as language learners all our lives. Spelling is not over in grade six. It should not just be demanded by secondary school teachers; it should be taught through writing, poetry, puzzles and games, reading, discussion and debate about words, linguistic exploration, study of second languages, and modelling by effective and affective teachers.

Gold stars are no reward for spelling growth. They are marks of praise for the short-term memories of students who have learned to play the game. I want my child to be instructed in spelling, to be taught, helped, enabled, informed, enriched by teachers who care about the whole of language. When I started teaching, I was a Dickensian archetype, but then Bill Moore entered my life as my language arts consultant, and opened up to me the riches of teaching and learning about words all the

131

time, not for only twenty minutes each morning, but every time we read or write, every time we sing or play, every time we laugh at a joke. He taught me to question and challenge why words work as they do, to learn about their origins, to laugh at their incongruities, to marvel at their complexities, and wonder at their power. He was the finest of spelling teachers, and yet he never mentioned the subject of spelling during those years. I feel such pain when a teacher says, "I don't care what research shows, or what changes have occurred in the last fifty years of teaching. I know how to teach spelling, and I'm going to continue working this way." Imagine a dentist saying similar things about his profession to that same teacher sitting in his dental chair!

Laughing All the Way to the Word Bank

Alphabet books, counting books, books of verse, books full of word puzzles, books based on culturally significant sequences such as days of the week or months of the year, and books that use recurring patterns from one page to the next—all allow children to enter the print world with confidence. But I have a special love for humorous children's books. As children laugh at slapstick or nonsense, funny or exaggerated characters, or ridiculous situations, words and expressions pop up and jiggle the funny bone, and the letters, patterns, and refrains remain in the children's long-term memories.

Children love puns and expressions that conjure up amusing images. Riddle and joke books are excellent resources for integrating listening and speaking with reading and writing. Starting the year with such word play, perhaps by pairing children to read a joke book together and then create their own riddle and joke books to share with others, shows them that words and how they go together will be an interesting focus for learning.

Many jokes and riddles hinge on the irregular correspondence between letters and sounds in English, and draw children into careful readings to discriminate between discrepancies. A number of jokes and riddles involve homographs (words that are spelled the same but differ in meaning, origin, and often pronunciation), or homophones (words that sound alike but differ in meaning, origin, and sometimes spelling).

Encouraging the use of tongue twisters in the classroom actively involves children in playing with words and enjoying the sounds of the language. Like joke, riddle, and pun books, collections of tongue twisters provide reasons for reading, encouraging auditory and visual discrimination and physical articulation.

Playing Our Way into Word Power

Games belong at the heart of childhood, and they help us remember the child in each of us. When we, as grown-ups, engage in play, we can often free ourselves from many of the restrictive behaviours we have imposed on ourselves over the years, and in doing so we find ourselves released into new learning.

Because games belong to the world of the child, we must be careful in using them for purposes of directed learning. Perhaps we can harness the energy of play for the business of learning, but it must not be at the expense of the spirit of the game. Games can't be used all the time to teach all things, but they can be a medium for altering attitudes and abilities in safe, enjoyable contexts. Often games require players to plan strategies, use memory, make decisions, solve problems, suggest alternatives, recognize patterns, analyze and synthesize, sequence, and evaluate. Depending on how it is used, a particular game can promote different areas of growth. Games can teach children to apply rules, give and follow directions, understand cause and effect, detect irregularities, weigh possibilities,

133

and generate possibilities. Games work from inside the children's world, propelling them towards discovery and creativity, building skills along the way.

Computers, in one form or another, are a part of the daily lives of many children. There are hundreds of games that can be played on screen using the internet or prepared programs. With the computer, children can search for and discover several games, then make a "game plan" for others to follow, keeping track of the results or printing the outcomes.

Board games such as Pictionary and Scrabble, which involve reading, spelling, and co-operative skills, can motivate children and encourage learning, and can also be used in co-operative learning lessons to encourage working in groups. Summer cottages are made for board games, on the porch, with family and friends, laughing our way into word power. (Couldn't we find time for word games in school?)

10. Turn printed texts into active learning.

Variations on a Theme

The novel *Nothing but the Truth* by Avi includes a variety of text forms, and provides a rich supply of issues for students to role-play:

- The ninth-grade boy being suspended for singing the national anthem, rather than standing silently by his desk;
- The boy telling his parents, who complain to the principal;
- The vice-principal talking to the teacher about her overreaction;
- The track coach trying to help the boy apologize and get back into school;
- The boy's friends discussing the whole affair;
- The teacher phoning her sister for support;
- And dozens of other stimuli for role-playing.

Watching students improvise from a story they have read helps me see their understanding of the text in front of my eyes. As they struggle to engage in the role-playing of the situations drawn from the story, or incidents that parallel the narrative, students are working from inside the author's ideas, to analyze

135

what has happened and to try to make sense out of it by engaging in dialogue with a partner or a group through role play, creating or recreating an incident or a conversation as if it were happening at that moment.

I am so heartened when I read Jeffrey Wilhelm's books on "active learning." We would call his strategies drama, but the activities are the same whatever we call them. We want youngsters to step inside the texts they read, to see the other sides of the words, to really see what's between the lines by owning the text. Through improvising and reading aloud, the students garner new perceptions and often connect their emotions to the ideas represented in the texts. When teaching any type of selection, I move quickly into active exploration—it makes my job much easier when the students drive the work.

Recently, I watched a group of university students in Jamaica present a play they had improvised from documents and letters chronicling the tragic story of a young woman who was captured into slavery and taken by ship to the Americas.

The students role-played different genders, different characters—from slaves to British judges—and through their dialogue, their dancing, and their ensemble choral work, they brought to life the complexities of the time, the injustice, the sadness, the history of their nation. I was deeply moved by their production, I learned so much about their stories, and I witnessed the power of action-based literacy education. If only all young people could use difficult text resources as material for literacy exploration, where through discussion and role-playing they could dig into the ideas, and struggle to understand the context and the times represented in the resources, as they work and rework their attempts to construct a drama form for their interpretations of the text!

Could we sing and dance our way into literacy?

The School Assembly

At 11.00 a.m. on November 11th last year, my son and I stopped what we were doing and observed two minutes of silence in our home. Remembrance Day has always been of great significance in my life, mainly because I was responsible for the school assemblies for so many years, and this particular occasion required a very specific approach on the part of the participants, in order to mark the solemnity with hundreds of young, sometimes restless people.

For one assembly, the children read war poetry while a young man played harmonica in the background. The "gymnatorium" actually became, for a few moments, a theatre, and everyone made an emotional connection. Afterwards, my inspector, who had been present, commented on my choice of songs, noting that "The Battle Hymn of the Republic" was identified with the United States, and we were a Canadian school. He was, of course, correct, but after I'd spent two weeks in rehearsals, struggling to find material that might, just might, touch those adolescents, his words seemed like an attack, and my spirits fell. I wish I could tell him now that I have found so many Canadian resources to use with our children, but he has long since left us. We teachers remember criticism for a long time, it seems. I shall put this one away now, and let the inspector rest in Canadian peace.

I first taught drama in a working-class neighbourhood full of people who were proud of their tiny homes, believed in the union, went to family cottages in the summer, and supported schools as the future hope for their children. I loved working there. The special parents' evenings we held to showcase our productions, having polished them and added sets and music, were community events, sold out, full of adults and children and babies, as close to the theatre of Shakespeare's time as any theatre event I have known. Since I had almost no drama background, I was constantly seeking songs, scripts, poems, and

137

skits that we could turn into an assembly program. One summer, while visiting London, England, I saw the musical *Oliver*, and bought the record. That fall in school, we read Dickens's novel and improvised a series of scenes, linking them with songs from the professional play. When we presented the work, it was a huge success. Humble though it was, it was that school's first experience with a Broadway-style musical. After our first performance, I was called onstage, where the principal asked the audience to give me a standing ovation for writing these marvellous songs, and I couldn't confess in front of all those cheering people who really were the composers. I don't know if they ever found out.

During the sixties, I moved to a new school, a junior high in a different socio-economic area. What a shock to find a school where, on some Wednesday afternoons, most of my classes were empty, the students having gone with their parents to the theatre matinees in Toronto. (I remember feeling so unworldly and unsophisticated, since I had seen only one play in my life, on a school outing to Niagara Falls for a production of *Hamlet*. The last scene with all the deaths, one on top of the other literally caused such laughter among the audience that we gave the production a rave review.)

The next month, I organized an excursion with my classes to *Annie Get Your Gun* with Ethel Merman, and the theatre world opened up and my life changed. Who ever thought that I would thank her for a career in drama?

Assemblies at this new school were artistic adventures in which some children brought in scripts they had performed at summer camp, some wrote their own plays, and others created improvised scenes. I learned much of what I now know from my early experiences with those children. John and Ira, aged fourteen, wrote a three-act spoof of the James Bond movie *Dr. No*, in which fifty adolescents parodied every aspect with such glee and finesse that we had to play it for the parents again and again. The staff, however, petitioned the principal because of a scene the young authors had created in which Dr. No Nothing, disguised as Santa Clause, was captured and forced to raise his hands, causing his pants to fall down, revealing his basketball shorts. The public code of decency had been breached, many teachers felt, but parental pressure can be a welcome force when it is on your side, and the principal allowed the show to continue. Today there wouldn't be a ripple of protest.

Scripts, written by students; literacy events where the words of one student group are read aloud by another; automatic revision and editing. Why are we so hesitant to incorporate scripts into our literacy programs? The involvement is instant; the literacy growth immediate.

Reading the War

My saddest moment in this school unfortunately concerned a Remembrance Day service. Because of anti-Vietnam war protests, I became nervous about focusing on the fighting and death inherent in all wars, so, using a United Nations script suggestion, I organized a program built around the theme of peace. I invited two gifted young folksingers from my previous school, who sang and played in the style of Simon and Garfunkle, to perform songs of hope for our young audiences, along with the UN-sponsored play built around the theme of peacemaking. It is such a thrill for a teacher to see former students successfully in action, and these boys did a fine job. The Scouts and Guides laid wreaths on a cross on the stage, but that was not enough to placate the staff members who had lost relatives in the two world wars, and another petition arose, labelling me a "peacenik." My principal, a war veteran, did his best to rescue me, but at the end of the year, it was time to move on.

I still see a few students from both those schools, and even though they are now in their fifties, I remember the dramas we built together, the children forever frozen in time as hope-filled adolescents.

However, this day when we commemorate soldiers haunts me. In 1976, I sent a class of graduate teachers who were enrolled in a course on drama in education to interview world war veterans who had spent their remaining years in hospital, some for decades. We were going to incorporate the stories they told into our drama explorations. This seemed to me a suitable way to prepare for the upcoming day, and to share strategies that they could then use in their classrooms. Of course, what they learned was not what I had intended.

They came back to class the next week full of frustration, and our discussions revealed that their source of anger was the ex-soldiers themselves. The stories they had recounted described their exploits all right, but they also revealed the pride they felt in having served their country, the camaraderie of men trapped together by conditions beyond their control, and the hatred they still felt towards the enemy. There was no contrition evident in these men who had had no home outside the veterans' hospital since being injured in war, no sadness about what war does to the human soul, just memories of a time when their lives meant more than the sum of all these institutionalized years. They faced the teachers with only their tales, no bodies to speak of, defiant in their fall from grace. But these teachers were from another time, born in the sixties and seventies of anti-war movements, of television newsreels of military atrocities, of university professors who had come to Canada as draft dodgers during the Vietnam war. They wanted nothing to do with these leftover warriors who made no apologies for their part in the past. But we know as literacy teachers that we read what our lives tell us to read; the meanings surround us where we live, and it is difficult to break through.

Why weren't these men ashamed, my students asked? Why weren't they aware of their part in the history of death? Why wouldn't they listen to these young teachers who felt that they alone had discovered the truth of how humans need to interact with each other? They had returned with stories that, in their eyes, shouldn't be heard, but we did explore them in our university classroom, role-playing those wounded shadows, and attempting to understand the reasons for the tales, the incongruity of the tellings, and the rejection by the told. I don't know what was learned, but this year I happened to be at a private secondary school during its Remembrance Day service, and who could not be moved by the solemnity of the music ensemble, by the poems of the students, by the words of the guests, and by the final procession when the student body proceeded past the guests, in single file, silent? Such a deeply moving literacy event. Why do the privileged seem to understand the necessity for ritual and ceremony? Why weren't those teachers from my course present? And does anyone left remember my cousin, Corporal Jackie Ross, who was killed in battle in 1944? Where are the Boy Scouts when you need them?

11. Focus on literacy in every subject.

Don't Know Much about Biology

My chemistry teacher in twelfth grade, Mrs. Brennan, understood how literacy worked, and she was certainly a scientist, in love with her discipline. In her class, following her ten-minute introduction to the topic, we students would first work in groups of four, carrying out an experiment. I always joined Joe Kormos's group, because he had no fear of the Bunsen burner, and I did. We would chat as we worked through the instructions, mixing and heating and pouring and combining, all the while taking notes. Next, a member from each group would write the observations on the blackboard, and Mrs. Brennan would take from each report items for a final draft, which we would then record in our notebooks, to be accompanied by a detailed diagram of the process, drawn in India ink so as not to be ruined by moisture, as a homework assignment. She never gave above a B+ for anyone's drawing, but I was determined to get an A. On my last diagram of the course, my paper was returned with a B++. A type of victory.

Like the wonderful Mrs. Brennan, I want students to be constantly engaged in the literacy events of every discipline—discussing, reading, writing, diagramming, researching, interpreting, representing, and shaping information, and then

143

sharing, presenting, arguing, refining, questioning, critiquing, summarizing, and responding to each other's findings and opinions, and revisiting, rewriting, revising, rethinking, reworking what we thought we knew. With younger children, the curriculum guides hold only touches and traces of what lies ahead, but I have watched youngsters begin to invest in these multiple ways of exploring the world, from kindergarten to twelfth grade, as they begin to work with the themes, issues, and concepts, along with the concerns, misconceptions, and surprises that inquiry holds. Every teacher has felt those moments of awe and wonder as students melt into the learning. What is new learning for the students can be satisfaction, even joy, for the teacher; we will watch them advance toward new and deeper understandings only if the teaching/leaning event has significance for their lives.

I remember visiting a school where the principal had organized a large science room for the fourth-, fifth-, and sixth-grade students. He told me that he felt his school-wide literacy program was weak, yet he had this amazing science teacher. Each class visited the science room for an hour three times a week, and I saw more literacy activity in that room than I have seen in many language arts rooms. The program was planned with exceeding care: starting a new theme each week, the children signed up for and worked in small groups at established centres, well supplied with all types of resources. They had to follow assignment cards at each work station and present their findings at the end of the third period. The room was always buzzing, and everyone was working. The teacher monitored and assisted where necessary, and group roles were assigned. The expectations were high, and I witnessed collaborative behaviours everywhere. There are times when planning and organization encourage and increase literacy growth, no matter what the subject. This is one such program.

We can only hope that students will want to behave as learners because the learning really matters to them and to the members of their learning communities. They will need to use the strategies that literate learners employ as they struggle to construct meaning. What is really exciting about a literacy community is that what we discover as a group usually exceeds what each of us could have achieved alone in our classroom. Individual students are shocked and surprised into knowing. During a reading of *Piggy Book* by Anthony Browne, in which a distressed mother who works outside the home finally abandons her husband and two boys because no one will help her with any of the household chores, a grade six boy responded aloud with "What a stupid mother!" Immediately, a young girl turned and said to him: "There's only one person who's stupid, and it's you." And for forty minutes, they debated the mother's desertion, each child learning through the dialogue with the other. The rest of us watched, and as participants we shunted between the two opinions, searching for informed ideas that could add weight to our own thoughts. The boy was shaken to learn that his ideas were to be challenged, but he opened his mind and began to shade his world in more subtle colours. The girl learned to gather and articulate her thoughts, to move beyond stereotypical responses to complicated questions. Ignorance isn't bliss; it's naivete and misinformation and hesitancy and fear and stubbornness, and much of it can be altered within the framework of school if we remember what schooling can and should do. We are aware of how the minds of our students construct and reconstruct their burgeoning world knowledge. We want them to become, like ourselves, involved in understanding the different literacy forms and requirements of the various disciplines in order to apply these learnings to their own problem-solving and decision-making endeavours.

Project Pain

School projects bring out the best and the worst in all of us. Teachers are convinced that projects are useful in the education of their students; parents know they will end up doing them; children don't think about them until the night before they are due. I have been involved in these nasty things for over fifty years, as child, teacher, and parent. In every instance, my hair curls at the memories. The autumn meant a leaf collection, and a leaf collection meant trying to find unusual specimens to raise my grade. Running around town searching for an oak tree was hard enough, but where could anyone locate an alder? We struggled to iron with wax papers our wide variety of samples, mount them on cardboard, and then carry them to school to meet the deadline. Of course, one year, on the day of reckoning it rained, and I arrived in the classroom with a spotted and blurred leaf collection. Do teachers know what it feels like to receive a B because it rained? What was the goal of my teacher's exercise, and why does it matter to me so many years later?

I had mocked leaf collections with that story so frequently in my classes that one fall morning, Gord Bennett, the science teacher at my faculty of education, visited my classroom with a huge green garbage bag full of wet leaves which he proceeded to dump on my desk while both of us laughed. He had heard my message, all right, and thought he would drive home his. What a fine teacher he was, and he understood so well what a project could or couldn't be. His student teachers found his classes full of science excitement that couldn't be contained on a piece of cardboard.

As the new young teacher of drama in a grade seven and eight school, I taught eight classes a day on a rotary timetable. I was expected to assign a project to the students each term, and I decided to ask them to build models of a Greek theatre. I had never been to Greece and these children from a working-class neighbourhood had never been to the theatre in any country,

146

but away they went with their projects. I had developed no guidelines, no checkpoints, no assessment strategies, to assist them, just a crudely copied picture of a model of a theatre in Athens. But this was a special school community, and the hard-working parents demanded that their children work just as hard so that they could move up the ladder—school projects were on the "must do" list. On the deadline day, of course, much to my chagrin, 640 students arrived at school with their models of Greek theatres, made from two-by-fours, cardboard boxes, balsa wood, and other material available for free from the spaces behind garages in back lanes. There was no place to put them, so they ended up in the hallways, on the staircases, in the basement—wherever there was a space. What a mess! But I still remember the pride on the faces of those parents who had helped transport the models to school—models many of them had probably constructed themselves. Culture with a capital C had finally arrived at their school and they welcomed it. I learned everything I know and believe about school projects that day, but most of all I remember my principal saying nothing. He knew the lesson had been learned, by both the students and their teacher.

I'm reminded of—and a little shamed by—my own father's role in a particular school project when I was in third grade. For three months I had been ill and absent from school, and on my return was notified of the twelve art projects that were due if I wanted to pass. In despair, I told my father and he hatched a plan: if I found out from the other children the types of projects that were required, he would complete them while I went on with my regular work. And he did. Sitting at the kitchen table, he drew and painted and printed and designed until they were all done. Then I took them to school. They were fine examples of a grade three student's work, and on parents' evening, each of those pieces of artwork was mounted on the walls of our little classroom. All our relatives came for the viewing, and it would be my father's first and last gallery showing. By coincidence, I wound up working at that school during my first year of teaching, and you may not believe it, but there above the blackboard, too high to reach, was a painting of two mittens my father had made, still on display all those years later. Some art lives forever.

And yet the role I played in my son's projects was very similar. At 8:00 on a Sunday evening when he was in high school, Jay announced that he had to build a small aquarium and have it ready for science class the next morning. It is comforting to know that many children behave in similar ways, but on that evening, my blood pressure forced me to come up with a plan. "Get in the car," I barked, and we drove to a Chinese restaurant where I proceeded to purchase several live fish from the tank. At home, we rinsed out a dill pickle bottle, added water, some fish, and a few Christmas decorations, and the next morning he met with success on his final project. At that moment, I resigned as project manager of anything to do with school activities of this nature, unless you count the nine essays with which I have assisted Jay over the next few years, just, you know, doing a bit of research, revising, editing, typing, illustrating, and hounding him to meet the deadlines. I think I have come a long way in letting him grow and work independently. I wish he thought so too.

Just think how references are changing. Even *Encyclopaedia Britannica* has moved to the CD-Rom as well as books, with subjects updated daily, and revised biweekly by 100 editors and 5,000 expert collaborators. And I find myself making frequent use of Wikipedia, a free online encyclopedia growing by leaps and bounds. The electronic dictionaries and other references are so simple to find that I am hooked. Plugged in forever.

Adding and Subtracting Our Way to Literacy

My high-school math teacher would try to solve the math puzzle in the morning newspaper each morning before our class began. He loved his discipline, and told stories of its use in his fighter pilot training during World War II. I remember him forty years later.

When we talk about "literacy" in the mathematics program in elementary schools, we are faced with different but interconnecting questions about teaching and learning: how are we defining literacy in our practice and theory, and how should we go about implementing literacy in our mathematics program so that the children will benefit? Today, as educators, we have come to understand that there are multiple literacies: we humans have found a variety of ways to make shared meaning in our lives—language, of course (both oral and written), music, art, dance, and all the symbol systems using mathematical concepts. For young people today, learning will require lots of opportunities to explore meaning-making with many of these forms, and in new combinations of them, such as the visual text literacies found in their electronic, computer-filled world.

Learning with and through mathematics means that youngsters are engaging in thinking processes using the codes of mathematics to test hypotheses and carry out inquiries, as well as traditional language codes that will enable them to consider, structure, and share the connections they are making. Students are thinking multi-modally, using two or more meaning-making systems (and they may be charting and diagramming their constructs along the way in a visual representation pattern). Becoming literate in mathematics, then, involves new ways of learning and knowing that will give children access to the technology and structure of mathematics so that they can analyze and interpret its problems and productions.

And yet there is another aspect of this particular world of learning that children will need to participate in as mathematics practitioners, and that is talking about mathematics. They will need to explore and communicate their mathematical thinking through talking and writing about the ideas and concepts they have been working with, to make connections between what they already know and what they are learning. By reflecting on their experiences in mathematics, they come to recognize and retain appropriate problem-solving strategies that they can use in the challenges they will meet. They come to see themselves working as mathematicians do, organizing, describing, recording, and reflecting about mathematical concepts and structures.

Students require information and experience in both language and mathematical modes of meaning-making, and especially in the interconnecting of these ways of representing ideas. They will need to be accomplished readers and interpreters of both types of texts; often some children are unable to handle tests and exams in mathematics because their language skills are too limited, even though they may have developed the requisite mathematical abilities. We will need to ensure that children's reading and writing processes are developing alongside their mathematical understandings, connecting them as often as possible in our classroom learning experiences.

It is, however, possible to go too far: in an attempt to make math relevant, I once asked my eighth-grade students to work out how much interest their parents would pay on the remaining years of their mortgage. I received thirty-two letters suggesting that this information was none of my business, and that there must be other ways to teach math. That is why some math teachers have red faces.

My friend Willa taught me a simple strategy for helping students understand those complicated math problems. Remember how the first pages in each chapter of the math book were just number exercises, but then you were hit with the dreaded word problems. How strange that we didn't see these as literacy issues back then. In fact we had the two literacies, two meaning-making codes—numbers and words. As a student, I seldom understood how to process those statements, but as a teacher, I had the answers in the manual. (I am not sure we are teaching mathematical concepts if we as teachers need an answer sheet.) Well, Willa taught me to read the questions out loud with the children, until the statements were clear in the children's minds. They could help each other explain difficult terms, or determine what was being asked. They were part of the class demonstration of how these two literacies work together, and as they came to understand the types of questions, they could proceed with the activity without the oral component. Some students will take more time than others to understand what is required in a question, but the numeracy component will get clearer and clearer. What if the problem all along for some children was always the word sentences, not the number sentences? How would we live with the guilt?

12. Welcome kids into the culture of literacy.

Only the Rich Can Read

I was going through customs from Canada to Washington, DC, a nerve-wracking task at best. When the burly young officer asked me why I was entering the States, I said I was going to attend a literacy conference. He asked: "What's literacy?"

I tried to explain that it concerned helping children become readers, whereupon he responded with a shattering statement:

"Reading? Only rich people can do that!"

I tried to explain that reading is a process that can apply to a variety of texts, but he just told me to move along.

What did he mean? Since he wasn't joking, was he referring to the cost of books, to the leisure time required to read, to a culture that supports occasions for reading, to the status that reading offers others but not him? Who did this to him? His school? His peer group? His family? How can we help him redefine his understanding of "reading"? His attitude disturbed and saddened me.

Books weren't separate from any of my other life experiences; they were part of them. I read because I wanted to read or be entertained or see another place or time. Books for me weren't on a special bookshelf; they were simply part of every daily event. We teachers make jokes about "reading reading" and "writing writing" (inauthentic tasks). But I know that we read for a reason and write for a reason. They have to be pretty authentic reasons or it doesn't work. I've worked with many doctoral students, and the ones who have something to say are easy to work with; the others have to learn how to find something to say. The ability to pick up a pen or a mouse doesn't make them writers. We have to work so hard to read and interpret what we really want to explore, find out about, share with others; it is not a simple process. A literacy event has to be organic, a significant activity, or it won't have lifelong impact.

Being literate means you can choose where you want to go in life. Education is about having more choices. If you aren't literate in a variety of texts, you are cut off from so much. I meet people who have no background in literacy. They haven't any ideas about how different print functions, which print text you can make sense of, or how to go about finding print text that works. They're just not at ease with much print text. The more literacy experiences we can give students, the stronger their understanding of how the texts work. Then their literacy passport is stamped and, of course, literature can open up for them.

I think of a child getting into the lake or the pool or the ocean and feeling at one with that medium, as mentors help him lift his arms more effectively, or help him learn to dive; that is the image I want for teaching kids with texts. With the water, you are always inside the medium, always interacting with the medium in a real way. We are looking at a story not because we have a guidebook, or coming along afterwards to see what we should have thought about the story, but because we're in that story full blast, and the mentor is going to help us swim inside that story and notice all the things underwater; at the edge of the pool, on the sand on the bank. I remember a woman in Vancouver taught me about noticing the items that are washed up by the ocean every morning. I hadn't noticed any of them before then. Another friend taught me to look up on Yonge Street in Toronto, so that I could see the lake amid all the buildings. I hadn't noticed that before. I am totally in favour of mentors and wish teachers would see themselves in that role, strong mentors, caring and believing in how children live and breathe and work and learn. I think that pools and beaches are great metaphors for school. Our kids will practise if they are somehow "with the water."

I really think if you want to get to know the real town, you have to know all the territory around it. Otherwise, it is like going to Brazil and living in your hotel in Ipanema, and not knowing there are millions of poor people living in favelas (slums). I am really interested in what we can do if we wander around and let ourselves wonder as we wander, with a guide who can point out things that we missed or didn't notice. Those are the journeys that I think reading teachers have to support.

What Does a Literacy Teacher Look Like?

Teacher, teacher, we don't care,
We can see your underwear.
Is it black or is it white,
Oh my gosh, it's dynamite!

There are so many jokes, stories, and rhymes in the lore of childhood about us teachers, but then, why wouldn't there be? Our students stare at us for five or six hours a day, two hundred days a year, for thirteen or so years. We must figure in some of their fantasies, or a few of their daydreams, as they wonder who and what we are really like outside these walls. Authors of books for children and youth readily draw upon these perceptions and misconceptions as background and atmosphere for their writings, even at times building a whole work of art around the teacher as the central character in a novel about the secret lives of schoolchildren.

155

How close to us as literacy teachers are the characters drawn from the imaginations and life experiences of the writers of children's literature? Do children build their images of us the way a writer creates a composite story teacher? When they grow up, what bits of us will be left in the toy box, what bits taken on the journey?

But rest assured: we teachers are part of the storytelling. Our teaching masks may slip in these tales of educational intrigue, but only to reveal hints and nuances of our whole beings. It may be true that we are what we teach, and that authors of books for young people weave their vague memories of school life into their stories—the good *and* the bad. The important thing is that we welcome kids into the literacy culture. Some of the novels mentioned can be read as cautionary tales: for even with the best of intentions, we can put potential readers off for a long time to come, if not a lifetime.

When we see a film or read books about us, about our worlds of education, we respond often with indignation or frustration. Is this who "they" think we are? I look carefully for myself as a teacher in the media daily, struggling to find out if the mirror lies. Do teachers truly welcome children into the literacy culture, or do they block the entrance?

I remember my grade nine English teacher so well, a mysterious woman who wore the same black dress all year, until Easter, when she appeared in a bright pink floral outfit, to the silent cheers of the whole class. Those eyes that stare notice when we get new contact lenses, when Miss Clairol visits or when sadness takes over our lives for a while. Bits and pieces of our personas are exposed as we teach, and slivers of stories enter the myths of the playground. I have come to value our appearances in the literature that children encounter. (My son did indeed have a teacher who lived in the school basement.) On the whole, we are portrayed as sensible taskmasters, sometimes exaggerated and silly, but usually supportive of the children involved in the tale. However, once in a while, I am brought up short as the fictional teacher behaves in ways that resonate with difficult truths I have read about or witnessed, or buried in my own mistake-riddled past, and these examples can serve as warnings for the consequences that arise from forgetting the complexities involved in working alongside children. In her book of poems, *I Gave My Mom a Castle*, Jean Little reminds us of the effects of careless teaching, from Valentine parties where one student receives none, to Mother's Day card-making with a motherless child. And, of course, Robert Cormier in *The Chocolate War* describes school commitment gone berserk.

The history of school stories is centuries old, beginning in England with Thomas Hughes's *Tom Brown's School Days*, as chronicled in the new edition of the *Norton Anthology of Children's Literature* (some 3,000 pages long). The genre was distinguished by the differences between male and female education, by friendships, bullies, manly boys, tomboys, the inspiring teacher's speech, showdowns in the principal's office, dramatic rescues, and moral dilemmas. After World War II, the portrayal of schoolchildren and their teachers became more realistic, even in parody. In Andrew Clements's *The Landry News*, a fifth-grade student complains about her burned-out teacher who, for a while, simply reads the newspaper all day. (I asked a boy who was describing this book to me if the teacher represented only fictional characters, and he replied with a twinkle in his eye, "Sometimes.")

We mustn't forget the setting of the widely popular Harry Potter books in a school with its own conventions, fantastical though they may be. As a teacher, I enjoy sharing the foibles and fractures of our daily lives in school with the students, teachers, and parents I meet. Somehow laughing at ourselves creates more opportunities for honest dialogue between the adults supervising the lives of children.

It may take artists to help us find ways of coping with all the complexities of schools today. Take the testing procedures facing all of us in schooling: can they help us to remember that assessment is there to assist us in making life better for the students, so that we don't fall prey to designing schools like the fictional Whittaker Magnet School, where "standardized testing truly is the work of the devil." It boasts the highest test scores in the nation, but at what price? "The classes are held in dreary, windowless rooms and students are force-fed noxious protein shakes to improve their test performance." Does the author, Edward Bloor, have a crystal ball, or is his book *Story Time* just a flight of fancy?

It hit a little close to home when I read that Margaret Narwin, the ninth-grade teacher in Avi's *Nothing but the Truth*, was considering taking a summer course in whole language because she found herself unable to relate to the young people in her English classroom. How dare an author of books for young people move onto my professional turf! And yet, during my career, I've found bits and pieces of myself in hundreds of teachers in children's books. This time, the image stared back at me from the page and I couldn't look away.

Have I been as unaware of my students as the experimenters who flashed phonics on a screen in Robert O'Brien's *Mrs. Frisbee and The Rats of NIMH* (in which the rats learn much faster than their instructors suspected and soon begin decoding the notes written for the lab technicians)? Did I assign book reports as a young teacher? Does my son have to do book reports now? In *Dear Mr. Henshaw*, Beverly Cleary slams the book report again and again as Leigh Botts reports on the same book for four years in a row. Was I sure I knew the newest and best system for teaching, without reference to my students? In Harper Lee's *To Kill a Mockingbird*, Miss Caroline Fisher taught Scout's class, ignoring the knowledge and advice of her students because, as Scout's brother Jem pointed out, she was teaching by the Dewey Decimal System.

Who are the teachers, anyway? In Virginia Hamilton's *The Planet of Junior Brown*, it's the janitor, Mr. Pool, who helps Buddy Clark. (I remember the caretaker who taught me drama in grade eight. He had come to Canada after the war from England, where he had worked in the theatre. How lucky we were!) Katherine Paterson leads me across *The Bridge to Terabithia* to meet Miss Edmunds, who takes Jess to the Smithsonian on her own time, and alters his life forever.

Perhaps I'll retreat more than a century back to the prairies and look at the schoolroom through the eyes of Laura Ingalls Wilder. After all, I too boarded with a couple in my first two years of teaching as Laura does in *These Happy Golden Years*. But I did not suffer as she did when the school day ended: she had to go back to a home where the husband was abusive. And yet I know it happens in teachers' homes, in students' homes. Where shall we find the ideal setting for our teaching dreams?

These writers were children once, students in my classroom. What are they saying about schools and teachers and students? Would these stories be so gripping, for teacher as well as child, if there were not truth in them? And how would I know who I was if there were no more children—and writers—to tell me? When I recognize that truth, I'm already moving on. Yet my reality is still formed by these books that have been part of my life with schoolchildren, with teachers, and with my own son. I smart from the sharp jabs some writers have given me, but I'm soothed by the honeysweet images of teachers depicted by others.

I think I'll take my chances with Ernestine Blue in M. E. Kerr's *Is That You, Miss Blue?* Students at Charles, a conservative religious school, have their days brightened by her unusual yet effective teaching methods. However, when her own unorthodox relationship with Jesus begins to dominate her life, she's asked to leave, and the girls realize their enormous loss. As an adult, one of them recalls her years with Miss Blue, and like all of us who mourn the passing of a loved one, she conjures up her image in the crowds on the streets of New York and longs to be recognized in return: "Miss Blue," I say, "It's me. Is it really you?"

As literacy teachers, we find ourselves in story, as does everyone who looks. The picture is always slightly out of focus, and we have to adjust our rose-coloured glasses. For those of us in teacher education, looking in the mirrors of our classrooms and struggling to make out the often distorted reflections provided by the children—and the artists writing for the children—is our starting point for tomorrow. We must therefore read with the children and help our student teachers read with the children, noticing the story and the writer and the children and ourselves all at once. Or else who will conjure us up when we have made ourselves disappear?

Children and teenagers search through the stories they read looking for their misunderstood selves, appreciating authors who still see much of the school world through the eyes of childhood. As do we. After all, educator Jerome Bruner says that stories exist only when we somehow connect with them. I think it may help us as teachers to enter the fictional worlds of school stories, interpret the perceptions and viewpoints of those imaginary students and teachers, and examine the stereotypes/archetypes of our own iconic images. These stories can reveal much about the societies that surround them—the time frame, the cultural contexts. Today's narratives have gone beyond the school walls of the past and reflect everything happening inside and outside the place called school, where life goes on for hours without parents, but with us.

Twenty-Two Things That Twenty-Two Boys Taught Me

I had the good fortune to be allowed to interview twenty-two boys from first grade to sixth grade at one elementary school in an urban setting for a film I was making to be shown at a conference on boys and literacy. Over two days, I met the boys one by one and chatted with them about reading, writing, and classroom literacy events. During the interviews it took only a minute or two before the boys forgot the camera and focused on our conversation. I had no particular questions prearranged; I just tried to follow their leads as topics arose. It was an exhilarating two days, and the resulting video footage allowed the editor and me to structure the film around several main concepts. The statements that follow are the words of the boys as they talked about their literacy lives.

I had asked for boys at risk in literacy, but the school wisely requested that I film a range of boys with different abilities in order to truly represent the nature of the student body. But each time I watch the film, I'm always surprised by the boys' confidence and by the ease with which they talk openly to me. This school is a nurturing and exciting community; the library, the computer room, the art on the walls, and the collegiality of the teachers tell me as a visitor that children thrive here. The school culture welcomes the students, and the students and the teachers define the culture. The answers of the boys often surprised me, and made me realize that we seldom make use of the thoughts our clients share with us in building our practice. Here is a sampling of their responses.

1. "My father reads out loud to my brother and me every night before bed."
   "What is he reading now?"
   "*The Penguin Book of Norse Mythology.* He finished Harry Potter already."

2. "I go to the library every Saturday with my friends. We like hanging around there. We play on the computers and take out books."

3. "My favourite books are Manga and other graphic novels."

4. "The student teacher read stories out loud to us and she used a different voice for each of the characters."

5. "Boys read adventure books. And dangerous books. Girls read Barbie stories."

6. "My older brother reads the Bible."

7. "I think boys and girls read similar books."
   "Would you read a romance book?"
   "Yes, some day, when I'm ready."

8. "When I couldn't learn to read in second grade, my father taught me that summer with books from the library. He helped me with the hard words and never yelled."

9. "I like working in the computer room. We're making a zine right now about the Maya."

10. "My father reads the newspaper."
    "Which one?"
    "The Sri Lankan paper. But he also reads the English ones."

11. "My grandma lives upstairs. She reads romantic books. And sad ones."

12. "My teacher read us three novels already this year."

13. "I'm only allowed to play computer games on weekends."

14. "My friend and me wrote a story about a king who couldn't have children. He wouldn't have an heir. We sent it to a publisher, but we never heard back."

15. "My teacher read a funny book to us about lima beans. How silly!"

16. "My mother reads books for herself that I bring home from the school library."

17. "I just read *The Landry News* by Bruce Clements."
    "What's it about?"
    "It's about a teacher who is lazy and doesn't work hard for the students."
    "It must be fiction. Teachers aren't like that, are they?"
    "Some teachers."

18. "I work with my reading buddy in third grade. I listen to him read and I talk with him about the story. I help with hard words."

19. "I wrote a story about my village, about a Baba. You know, a seer who can tell your future by reading your hand."

20. "I'm not too good a reader and I have to do a book report every week. It's hard."

21. "I've read seventeen of the twenty books you need to read for the Silver Birch contest. You have to read different genres."

22. "Do you know any men who read?"
    (After a long pause…)
    "You."

Literacy Rituals and Ceremonies

My next door neighbour, Elija, is thirteen years old, and has just finished grade eight. He told me in June, with great excitement, that there was going to be a dinner, a dance, and a party for all the graduates. Of course, the elementary school leave-taking is a life-altering experience, and requires rituals. He is cutting my lawn every week to save money to buy a

163

laptop computer, a significant literacy ritual in many of our students' lives as they join the culture of the future.

At my son's graduation from grade eight, each of the graduates was honoured by a grade seven student who was a friend, and as each speaker recounted the time in the school of the honouree, he presented the graduate with a rose. All of the grade eight students were teary-eyed, as were teachers and parents. This ceremony marked the turn into adolescence for these youngsters, into high school, away from childhood. The biographical speeches, drawn from interviews and observations, were such a far cry from public speaking events relying on memorized data; this was an authentic occasion for sharing carefully crafted reflections concerning those who now would leave the circle of that school. A significant literacy event.

Schools need rituals. Each school building is a meeting place for hundreds of children. Rituals can help students and teachers to hang on to ways of behaving so that the group feels that it knows how to function in one space, and to function for good reason. Rules are different from rituals; they are seldom imbued with pride and ceremony. The past isn't felt, at least not as deeply. I like to visit schools where I see rituals and ceremonies. The students know how to belong, what membership entails, and why we all need to accept and value them. It is often difficult in a new building to begin the careful construction of what the past will now look like in the new surroundings, but begin it must, or there will be no sense of membership. Private schools have always known this, but I am seeing some great strides in the organization of meaningful customs in public schools throughout North America. How we greet guests; the entrance foyer; the auditorium meetings, the field day; the library; the awards day; leave-takings; speeches by officials; music night; and so on.

Perhaps literacy achievements need rituals, too All the following literacy events deserve a celebration, no matter how modest.

- The first book read by yourself in grade one or two demands a cake, or at the very least, a muffin;
- Reading your part in a script, and keeping up with the other readers—you have joined the literacy club;
- Mentoring a first-grade reader when you are in eighth grade, and witnessing the growth;
- Reading aloud to your grandmother when she is in hospital;
- Writing and performing your first song on the piano or guitar;
- Keeping a writing journal for an entire year;
- Emailing an author and receiving a response;
- Participating in a chat line with students from another school;
- Writing a poem and realizing it actually *is* a poem;
- Volunteering to work on the yearbook;
- Searching for automobile information on the internet and helping your parent select a car;
- Completing your first research project using interviews and the internet;
- Being able to read your grandmother's handwritten letter for the first time;
- Finishing a novel, and feeling sad that it was over.

What would you add to the list?

Writing this has triggered my memory of one of my first school graduation ceremonies: as a first-year teacher of fifth grade, I witnessed the pomp and ceremony of sixth graders marching up to the gym stage to receive their diplomas, as they prepared to leave for junior high. The entire gym was filled with vases of roses gathered from the gardens of the comfortable middle-class homes surrounding the school. I was amazed at the work and the care that the teachers and parents had put into this ceremony, and as a naive young teacher, I considered the event overdone. Now, of course, I yearn to see a gym filled with flowers from nearby gardens as children watch their brothers and sisters depart for the next phase of the journey. Last year, I did observe a friend's daughter graduate from secondary school, and the event was held in a large church, echoing with all kinds of rituals. Once again, the speeches by the students were carefully crafted, with just the right touches of humour and sentiment. As well, they had created an elaborate program, filled with stories of students past and present, writing and reading that mattered to everyone in the audience. Liturgical literacy.

My son came home from summer camp at fourteen, filled with all kinds of teenage anecdotes about living in the wilds with 200 adolescents, but the one that stood out concerned the ritual of the last day. He told how the counsellors paddled the canoes to the middle of the lake and lit torches, while those on land chose a stone from the beach that would be their memory rock of their time together. Then they sang the camp leave-taking song, and I could see in his young eyes that the co-operative ritual mattered. Imagine 200 young people focused on one emotional moment: does it sound like school? It could.

There's a Parent Peering in the Window!

When I began teaching, my principal told me to cover the window in the door with some paper, so that the parents couldn't see in. Now schools want to develop realistic collaborative goals for working alongside parents. By listening to parents, we can discover a great deal about the family literacy in their homes and incorporate that knowledge into the programs we develop for their children. We can increase communication during interviews or phone calls, or by a classroom newsletter, so that they are aware of how our program functions and can give appropriate support. We can discuss how to assist a troubled reader, why a child needs to read a book silently before sharing it aloud, how to chat with their child about reading and writing, how to find a quiet time for reading, how to extend the range of literacy events in the family setting with TV guides or by writing weekly menus, how to use the classroom and public libraries to locate books to read aloud (perhaps with a babysitter or older sibling). We need to involve parents wherever possible, without adding guilt or stress to their lives, in all aspects of their children's literacy progress, while remembering that they are not teachers, and that the reading and writing experiences at home should be natural and positive so that these children can be helped to work through their difficulties, not punished. Homework is often a troubling time for these students; we need to be aware of the demands we place on these children, and offer parents specific and clear suggestions towards understanding what is necessary to be achieved each night, and how those tasks will support the child's growth as a reader and a writer. We need to value parents as partners in creating a literacy culture.

Homework horrors have filled every home, and still, as teachers, we haven't figured it out. Some of us see the daily regimen as a necessary evil: we did it so why can't today's kids? Still others neither read nor assess the kids' accomplishments the next day. As society shifts, so do the demands we place on parents, and on children. I am arguing for a homework policy, a curriculum, if you like, worked out before we meet the children in the fall. We neither give work that requires a wise counsel by adults to be accomplished, nor set expectations that are destructive to the child's family's home life. Schools don't need to ask me how much homework to give; they need to take a good look at what is happening right now, suspend judgment, and do some research. What is working? What could work? How can we help make it work? Could we make a schedule with the class on Monday for the week, so everyone knows what is expected? In my opinion, the books sent home to be read to parents in primary grades have to be carefully monitored, or both parent and children will find reading the best books a chore, not a worthwhile experience. One school asked me about reading journals, to be completed every night after reading. If the activity creates negative learning, stop it! As a school community, find a different, better way of promoting independent reading. Most reading should be done in class, where there are teachers trained and prepared to help a child move towards literacy proficiency. We need to see homework activity as learning in its own right, not more of what we didn't understand in school. It needs to be accomplished in bite-sized chunks, each evening, so the pattern is established, but it needs to be achievable in a two-bedroom apartment with three children around the kitchen table, with two parents who have worked hard all day, with time for a Scout meeting, hockey practice, and some television. Learning how to accomplish school tasks at home is useful, if the task can be accomplished without the teacher.

Looking in the Rear-View Mirror

If you begin with your life as a teacher, all the other pieces fit into that framework because you use stories of your life, your own childhood, your teaching past, your teaching friendships, in your journey towards becoming a professional. I see myself as "teacher," and incorporate all the rest into how I teach the art form of my life called teaching. I tell stories about everything I have learned from my teaching to make my points, to draw my analogies, to build my other worlds. I think my son would see me as a teacher, too, because so much of my life is built around school.

I've changed my definition of literacy so much since my own childhood. Literacy for me is making meaning of any text we perceive, whether it's print or film or talking to an adult or a child. All are texts of our lives. To me, print text is only one kind of text. What interests me about print is that it's a kind of artificial text that has its own little sci-fi world and works in particular ways. Having children understand how the print text works is a very spectacular way of opening them up to a world frozen in time, where they can meet the authors of the ideas. Suddenly that print text, that artifact, can reveal how it was constructed. I enjoy talking about story because we "freeze" story. Then, we can add water and stir and wonder about who created that story, how that text appeared in this world, and where my life fits in with that story.

You don't have to be a teacher to know about literacy. I realize that when I talk about my son Jay, I am really talking about having the opportunity to observe a child growing for a long period of time; then I step back and notice what that all meant. Because you're part of it, you can think more deeply about it. But you can do that with Big Brothers or Big Sisters or relatives, and even effective teachers can be observers. If you teach kindergarten, follow your kids to the next grade and observe them over the next few years. Did you falter in your own stereotyping of them? Where did you go wrong? I wish we would, all of us, have opportunities to see kids growing over time. I observed my friend's daughter, Marah, in British Columbia for twenty-one years because I went out there every year to teach. It was like viewing a wonderful film. Every year she was taller, different, brighter, and better equipped to interact with me. I think I was able to do that with Jay as well because of my being a teacher. It let me peek at his growth in carefully controlled and obvious ways. I was fortunate that he was there. The thing about being a father is that you make so many mistakes and see the results of your mistakes all the time, whereas in teaching we

169

don't, because the students move on so quickly. Seeing a child over a period of time is the magic.

For those of us involved in literacy education, life in school can be a rich yet perilous quest for ways to guide and lead young people into a deeper understanding of themselves and their place in the world. At times we risk all that we value ourselves, as we work with our students inside the ever-evolving frame of the modes of texts, continuing to grow and change alongside the youngsters, sometimes voluntarily, but often carried into new realms of meaning-making by their energy and spirit, and their naïve and defiant refusal to accept our initial ideas as their truths. Our hidden assumptions and biases are fodder for their explorations, and their very self-focused attitudes and behaviours cause us to twist and turn with the anxiety borne in the sudden realization of where we have to journey with them next in order for something good to happen. And the most complex part of this process is that they must choose the path while we are so clear about the destination.

Like Coyote, I need to remember that I am a "shape-shifter," that I can adapt not only my tricks of the trade but my own persona in order to participate in some way in the experience. For the teachers I know and respect continue to enter the learning in their lives and in their work, living their professional lives, as British educator James Britton mentioned many years ago, as "spectators and participants," both at once, in our classrooms. We must find opportunities (it is an imperative for us who teach) to be active, visible members of the literacy culture, to continue reading and composing and designing on paper and computer; and sometimes this can occur alongside our students. But we educators teach all the while, observing with every inch of our beings, redirecting, encouraging, supporting, offering assistance, finding resources, sharing what we have found out, and marveling at what we have not yet discovered. We are both inside and outside the experience, benefiting from both spheres—risk-taking novices and astute professionals alike—enmeshed in the topsy-turvy endeavours of the psyche-stretching world of the complex and life-enabling literacies.

As someone involved in teacher education, I feel most fulfilled in my work when teachers and youngsters are participating in the same workshop together, growing alongside each other, freed from so many of life's expectations, feeling as equals with the experience. Dorothy Heathcote taught me this education principle many years ago in England, in a group session with teachers participating in her drama workshop that took place in a residence for severely mentally challenged girls. When teachers and students had gathered in the gym, Dorothy instructed the adults to "Choose a student partner, and join in the dance of spring," as a storyteller and musicians created the context for the age-old myth of Persephone. And my partner was Esther. She wore her wonderful red cowboy boots, and together we moved into the group creating Persephone's ritual of spring, "None of this modern dancing," Dorothy called out. "Just what happens as the two of you move into the story." And amid the flute and the tale and the sixty or so bodies in the room, Esther reminded me to remain in the moment at all times in my life, to allow myself the privilege of entering once again the world in the company of young people. When a child holds your hand, how can you be afraid?

I just noticed that my computer is covered with dust. My son learned in biology that 90 percent of the dust in our home consists of discarded human cells. I am covering my computer with my very skin; I am becoming my computer. How much of me is hidden there; will my DNA be found in my laptop when I am gone? I must confess that I give most of the books I acquire away now; I keep only those I want to re-read. I wish my desk were larger, so that my books and my computer could live happily together. I seem to need both in this new culture of literacy.

My friend Vicki Kelly reminds me that, "With books in Braille, the reader touches the words, and the words touch the reader." I would want all readers to feel the words, to be touched by them, to read and write their own sacred texts to house their spirits.

> What is the source of poetic light that illuminates the night of Homer's blindness? It is imagination, which is also important to common sight. The light of imagination will occupy half of our history, because of its significance for both the ancient world and poetry, and the present world and science. No matter how brilliant the day, if we lack the formative, artistic power of imagination, we become blind, both figuratively and literally. We need a light within as well as daylight without for vision: poetic or scientific, sublime or common.
>
> —Arthur Zajonc, *Catching the Light*

I was watching a man putting in a sewer on Broadway in Manhattan. I think of him working in 10 degrees below zero with no washroom nearby and no respect on the subway when he goes home in dirty clothes. I like to work equally as hard as that chap does, and my work happens to be with teachers, kids, and texts. I don't see it as hard work or as demanding all my hours. This is what I do and I will do it as long as I can, as hard as I can, just like the person who is flying the airplane, or collecting the refuse or handling all the office workers in that building next door. We are all workers, and my work is helping teachers and kids explore texts together. That has been my life's work, and I am grateful for it.

101 Literacy Events

These events are intended for kids, parents, teachers or all three.

1. Babies need books too! Read and sing and tell stories to them. Let them enjoy the pictures.
2. Read to your kids—stories, news, letters, poems.
3. Read *with* your kids, side by side, and as they read.
4. Let your kids read on their own: in the car, in bed, lying on the floor.
5. Play board games—at the kitchen table, on holidays, in the evening.
6. Notice *life print* around you—ads, signs, menus—and point out examples of word play.
7. Make tape recordings with your kids. Take parts, and add sound and music.
8. Let the kids read taped books. They can follow along with the text as they listen.
9. Sing songs with your kids. Share the lyrics.
10. Bus, train or plane trips are for reading, too. Put a bag of books and comics on board.
11. Kids need to collect things. Help them arrange and label each artifact.
12. Find the patterns in books—refrains, lists, completions, parallel sentences.
13. Read alphabet books together. Add your own different words for each letter.
14. Read and write letters to and from friends. Use interesting papers and pens and crayons.
15. Write and read emails. Print them out and make a booklet of them.
16. Download everything that matters.
17. Have the kids connect with an e-pal.
18. Have kids check references to questions that arise on the internet as often as possible.
19. Have kids reread part of a text to prove a point during discussions.
20. Let kids retell a story to own it.
21. Have kids rewrite a story in their own words.
22. Scribe for your kids when they tell you a story.
23. Ask kids to keep a list of the books they read.
24. Have your kids read twenty-five books a year.
25. Have kids read favourite poems aloud each day.

26. Read novels written as poems, such as *Out of the Dust* by Karen Hesse.
27. Let the kids read topical non-fiction articles and books.
28. Support the kids' reading of every book in a popular series.
29. Find out about favourite authors from the internet and the media.
30. Watch TV and films made from books with the kids.
31. Attend an author's talk, and share the experience with the kids.
32. Make the kids' homework an effective use of time; plan and organize what can be accomplished.
33. Make graphic organizers to support the process of writing.
34. Help the kids keep journals or notebooks of daily events and feelings, in a special book or on the computer.
35. Write a dialogue journal with your kids about what they are reading: they write, and you write back.
36. Let your kids read the mail: ads, brochures, sales, coupons, portions of letters.
37. Social studies and science are also about reading. Help kids learn how to read information materials, including on the internet.
38. Help kids read manuals to learn how things work.
39. Practise all types of tests. Make them funny, so that kids can learn about test structures (true/false, etc.).
40. Have kids read and circle their choices in the TV guide.
41. Let kids plan for and read maps on an excursion.
42. Kids can read aloud to younger buddies.
43. Kids can read aloud to older buddies.
44. Let kids paint and draw stories.
45. Make handwriting special with calligraphy pens and beautiful paper.
46. Explore different fonts on the computer. Pick a favourite.
47. Make all kinds of books for writing, from scrapbooks to homemade pop-ups.
48. Compare ads in the newspapers for similarities and differences in style and content.
49. Let different kids read different sections of the newspaper.
50. Provide free community papers for kids.
51. Read and write memos of thanks, apologies, and encouragement.
52. Keep bulletin boards up to date with materials that connect to school and home.
53. Read what kids in other places are reading by using surveys from schools on the internet.
54. Have the kids make overheads, charts, and Power Point presentations for different curriculum subjects.

55. Help kids to keep a word bank in a special book or on the computer: demon spelling words, words new to English, unusual words.
56. Help kids learn how words work, by playing word games, by noticing common roots and endings, and seeing patterns.
57. Create a "Word Wall" of words kids will need for a project.
58. Share your own background as a reader.
59. Build comprehension through real conversations about what the kids have read.
60. Let boys read what they want to read.
61. Let girls read what they want to read.
62. Find resources that both boys and girls like.
63. Read books together as a class community.
64. Let everyone read independently for a time.
65. Let kids read books that are connected by place or theme or time.
66. Model reading and writing events for the children every week. Show them how you work with a print text to build meaning. Include your own mistakes and revisions.
67. Invite a bunch of readers for lunch to discuss what they are reading.
68. Read a story with your kids, stop every so often, and have them predict what might happen next.
69. Share your opinion about a book a child has read supplemented by reviews or connected information.
70. Teach your kids to skim and scan for information on the internet.
71. Help kids connect their lives to the books they're reading.
72. Help kids connect the books they read to world issues.
73. Remember that computer screens are literacy tools.
74. Use the writing process to help kids construct their own significant compositions from their own interests.
75. Write a co-operative poem as a class, with kids suggesting words and lines.
76. Have kids illustrate their writing: older kids can make books for younger kids.
77. Teach kids to cut and paste as they revise and edit their writing.
78. Help kids learn how spelling works by teaching them about patterns, roots, and endings.
79. Punctuate sample texts from which the punctuation has been removed.
80. Help kids understand grammar so they can talk about language.
81. Libraries are free. Go with the kids.
82. Let kids read about places holy to their religion.
83. Create a timetable for focusing on reading and writing strategies.
84. Own your own books and talk about them and display them.

85. Interview your kids about what they're reading: videotape the conversation so you can both revisit the experience.
86. Book reports can kill reading. Use different techniques for promoting reading and deepening understanding.
87. Celebrate your literacy heritage by talking about special moments in your own family's reading events.
88. Laugh your way into literacy with joke books and cartoons.
89. Include pop culture in your reading resources.
90. Let kids find riddles you can't answer.
91. Develop computer zines with the kids.
92. Talk about bestsellers lists in the newspaper, and share what you would like to read. Find lists of bestsellers for kids on the internet.
93. List and talk about everything you have personally read for one whole week.
94. Encourage kids to role-play characters in a story.
95. Encourage emotional responses to a story through discussions.
96. Memorize a poem and say it aloud for the kids.
97. Read scripts out loud together.
98. Make scripts out of stories by combining the narration and the dialogue.
99. Let kids read aloud and share the stories and projects they have written.
100. Read a novel aloud while everyone follows along with their own copies.
101. Let kids find out everything they can about everything!
Trivia matters!